Building
Emotional
Intimacy in
Your Marriage

Achieving Closeness that Will Last Forever

Jeff and Florence Schachinger

Building Emotional Intimacy in Your Marriage

Building Emotional Intimacy in Your Marriage
© 2015 by Jeff and Florence Schachinger

All rights are reserved. No part of this book may be duplicated, copied, translated, reproduced or stored mechanically, digitally or electronically without specific, written permission of the author and publisher.

Previous ISBN: 978-157782282-0
New ISBN: 978-1-941988-00-8

Unless otherwise indicated, all Scripture references are from the Holy Bible, New International Version, copyright 1973, 1978, 1984, 2011 by the International Bible Society. Used by permission of Zondervan Bible Publishers.

Book cover design: Toney Mulhollan. Interior book design: Thais Gloor.

Illumination Publishers is committed to caring wisely for God's creation and uses recycled paper whenever possible.

About the authors: Jeff and Florence Schachinger make their hom in Southwest Connecticut where they are both in the full-time ministry with the Southern Connecticut Church of Christ. They have been married for thirty years and have two adult sons and a teenage daughter. They love teaching about marriage and family.

Illumination Publishers books may be purchased in bulk discounts for classroom instruction, retreats and promotional use. For additional information email us from our website at www.ipibooks.com.

www.ipibooks.com

To Taylor, Jonathon, and Fiona

We pray that God will lead you to
all the joy and fulfillment
in life that we have been able to find.

"Delight yourself in the Lord
and he will give you the desires of your heart."
Psalm 37:4

Contents

Introduction
Building Emotional Intimacy
more than you can imagine 9

1. **The Emotional Connection**
   God helps us build intimacy 17

2. **The Need for Acceptance**
   unconditional love brings safety 33

3. **I'm Going In**
   the challenge for men to go deeper 53

4. **Worth More Than a Ruby**
   being a noble wife to your husband 71

5. **Not Quickly Broken**
   the importance of spiritual intimacy 89

6. **Don't Settle for Less**
   having vision for your marriage 105

Introduction
Building Emotional Intimacy
more than you can imagine

> Now to him who is able to do immeasurably more than all we ask or imagine, according to his power that is at work within us...
>
> Ephesians 3:20

From Jeff

I know what you're thinking—what, another book on marriage? Do we really need another book on marriage? Hasn't it all been said? Haven't we heard enough?

Well, I guess that depends upon where you want to go in your marriage. Are you content with simply "staying the course," or do you have your sights set on new heights?

I've always wanted to be a pilot. The closest I've ever come is when I buzzed the Nashville skyline, my hands firmly at the controls of a friend's Cessna. (Don't worry; he was in the seat beside me, hands and feet at the ready!) With a little effort and a pull, you can orchestrate dramatic climbs!

In contrast, have you ever watched a glider in flight? They are different "birds." The thing about a glider is that it doesn't climb much. It has to be towed to its peak; then its entire time in the air is a slow descent back to earth. It may take a while, but eventually it comes down.

Which aircraft best describes your marriage? Are you pushing forward, pulling out the stops and climbing higher? Or do you feel like your marriage is on a slow descent and the ground is getting closer? Maybe it's not about to crash, but it's not exactly climbing either!

Not too long ago, I was definitely relating to the glider. But what I've learned about emotional intimacy has turned my marriage around 180 degrees, and I sincerely hope it will do the same for you.

At the time of this writing we have been married twenty-five years—quite a milestone in this age of "disposable marriage"—and I can honestly say that today I am more in love with my wife and more into my marriage than ever. I wasn't always able to say that. Let me go back about ten years.

By all accounts everything in our lives looked fine. We were busy raising our two boys, busy leading a ministry, busy with life. Nothing out of the ordinary. Your basic life pressures and responsibilities, but I would have these thoughts...these feelings..."Something isn't right here." I couldn't put my finger on it, but I knew something was missing. Our sexual relationship was strong, but we spent little time really talking with each other. I was busy with people and so was she.

After our third child was born, our together time was watching TV at night. After a few years I finally realized what it was...that missing piece. We had become emotionally detached. I knew I loved her; I just didn't always feel it. There were no bad feelings, just not enough good ones. We had an emotional void in our marriage.

There would be times when I would find my wife crying, unable to express what she was feeling. I felt frustrated and helpless. We had lost touch with each other's real needs, desires and hearts. Our marriage had become stale and tired, and we needed to do something about it. We had to get deeper and address areas of forgiveness, acceptance, grace, humility, honesty and patience. We needed to deal with things from the past and present.

We hung in there, determined to work on this, and God has brought us to a great place. A place with no walls, no barriers, no secrets, no games. An emotional bond we plan on keeping forever!

From Florence

"Oh, I really hope my husband will read this. He certainly needs help with connecting emotionally." Wives, this might be your first thought! But a warning here: I've learned how important it is to look into my own heart first, not to squelch my desires and thoughts, but to express them in a righteous manner. We both needed to learn how to be emotionally intimate.

This has been a journey filled with pain, joy and amazing rewards. I'm not writing as a professional marriage counselor, but as C.S. Lewis puts it: "Think of me as a fellow patient in the same hospital who, having been admitted a little earlier, could give some advice."[1]

I can say that I agree with Jeff's description of our marriage! We were in love, happy, no obvious problems. Some bumps from time to time, a seemingly "low maintenance" couple, but I can say now that we weren't completely honest with our deepest feelings and thoughts. Honesty brings potential conflict, and conflict—to me—wasn't good. (So not true, but that's how I felt.) I have memories of fighting back tears as we talked in the car or after having some interaction at home. I would tell myself, "You're fine; just forget about it," and make the decision that the conversation I was having in my head would never be said out loud.

Sometimes I would even hide my tears so I wouldn't have to explain why I was crying. I would tell myself, "You're too demanding emotionally; just stop expecting so much from this relationship."

As the stress of life continued to get more intense (death in the family, job loss, financial strain, spiritual testing), we were forced to face the void we were both feeling but not expressing to each other. We had to make the decision that our marriage being its best

---

[1]. Letter to Sheldon Vanauken on April 22, 1953. Quoted in *A Severe Mercy* (New York: HarperOne, 1987), 134.

was the priority God desired. It was imperative that we approach issues from a different angle.

We made promises to each other not to get defensive, to expand our listening capabilities, and to be free to express completely what we were feeling and thinking. We needed to push past the barriers that we had built without even realizing it.

Can you relate?

My eyes were opened to see how Satan wants to destroy our marriages in both obvious and subtle ways. It's amazing how free my heart now feels about my marriage. I'm so much in love with Jeff in a deeper, more emotionally intimate way, but it took a lot of work, a lot of tears, a lot of talking, and a lot of God's power. I understand Paul's words much better now: "To this end I labor, struggling with all his energy, which so powerfully works in me" (Colossians 1:29).

We realize that all of us are at different stages and in different places with our marriages. Some see the need for change right now; some may not. Some may be ready to dive right in, and some may want to stick a big toe in first!

Wherever you are, we want to encourage you to simply do the best you can at whatever pace you need to travel. Just stay with it and don't give up!

We really hope this book will help you find emotional intimacy in your marriage. Read the scriptures, and do the exercises together at the end of each chapter. Give it your all, and God will give *you* "more than you can imagine."

Blueprints for Intimacy

To get started, take some time with your spouse to discuss the following questions:

1. What made you fall in love with your spouse?

2. What do you feel are the top three strengths in your marriage? (both of you share)

3. What do you feel are the top three weaknesses?

4. What do you hope to gain by reading a book like this?

1

The Emotional Connection

God helps us build intimacy

He ordered one hamburger, one order of French fries and one drink. The old man unwrapped the plain hamburger and carefully cut it in half. He placed one half in front of his wife, then carefully counted out the fries, dividing them into two piles, and neatly placed one pile in front of his wife. He took a sip of the drink; his wife took a sip and then set the cup down between them.

As he began to eat his few bites of hamburger, the people around them kept looking over and whispering. You could tell they were thinking, "That poor old couple. All they can afford is one meal for the two of them."

As the man began to eat his fries, a young man came to the table, politely offering to buy another meal for the couple. The old man said they were just fine; they were used to sharing everything.

The people around them noticed the little old lady hadn't eaten a bite. She sat there watching her husband eat and occasionally taking turns sipping the drink.

Again the young man came over and begged them to let him buy another meal for them. This time the old woman said, "No, thank you. We are used to sharing everything."

As the old man finished and was wiping his face neatly with the napkin, the young man again came over to the little old lady who had yet to eat a single bite of food and asked, "What are you waiting for?"

She answered, "The teeth!"

Marriage Is All About Sharing

When God created all living things, there was no suitable helpmate to be found for Adam, so God took one of Adam's ribs and created a wife for him. Now that's sharing!

In Ephesians 5:31 the apostle Paul says about marriage: "for this reason a man will leave his father and mother and be united to his wife, and the two will become one flesh." He goes on to call it a "profound mystery," and we might well agree!

In your world of "one another" relationships, this is the most important one. "One flesh." God meant for there to be no separation in our marriages. A true partnership. But is this really possible? Do we see much of this kind of partnership in the world? No! In fact we see quite the opposite. There's a reason why we have such a high divorce rate. Becoming one and staying one takes something that many people are lacking, something they fear: emotional intimacy.

We believe the lack of this intimacy is the root of most marriage problems. It's the number one reason marriages become weak, dull, boring, stale and in trouble. We've seen it in old marriages and new marriages, and it's not part of God's design for your marriage. God has a plan for your marriage to grow, to mature and to be fulfilling in every way. He has a plan to make you happy and healthy for as long as you're both alive. His desire is for you to become one and stay forever one. That takes emotional intimacy!

What Exactly Is Emotional Intimacy?

Intimacy involves a relationship where the blinders come off and the walls come down. It's a relationship where you get real and you get close. We know for some that sounds scary, but isn't that what you really want in your marriage?

When contemplating how to subtitle this collection of thoughts, convictions and experiences in our marriage, we kept seeing the following scripture flash in our minds:

> Now to him who is able to do immeasurably more than all we ask or imagine, according to his power that is at work within us... (Ephesians 3:20)

God is such an incredible giver. He wants us to experience his gifts to the full extent. Our marriages are gifts to be treasured, protected and enjoyed! God is more than able to strengthen our marriages and to mold them into a "haven of intimacy." Maybe that's more than *you* can imagine right now, but we all need to ask God for his help. Down deep in our hearts, we desire intimacy, but do we allow ourselves to admit this God-given need?

As disciples of Jesus, we desire intimacy with God,

and we know the effort it takes to maintain it. The question is, are we willing to put that same effort into our marriage? In Ephesians 3 Paul is on his knees praying to his heavenly Father with a deep understanding of God's power and authority. He understood that God desires to bless his children. Paul understood that anything is possible through the Spirit in our inner being—"according to his power at work."

We need to be confident of this truth: his power is at work within us and within our marriages. It's imperative that we focus on the power and the depth of God's love, continually asking for his help so that we can experience what he *wants* us to experience, which is more than we can ask or imagine!

Now Is the Time

Having a relationship for thirty-one years that began completely separated from God and completely ignorant of his ways, we found that this scripture gave us the hope we needed. When we became disciples, it was more than we could have imagined, but that was only the beginning of a journey to find a greater understanding of intimacy with God and with each other.

Maybe you've been begging God for your marriage. Maybe you're disillusioned with how yours has turned out. Maybe you're feeling hopeless, completely unfulfilled. Or maybe yours is good, but you want more!

Wherever you are, the time to work on intimacy

is now! You can't afford to grow apart. How can you be the light of the world that God calls you to be if you're not satisfied and shining bright at home? That's why you must do all you can to build an emotional connection, a true emotional intimacy.

You may have questions and concerns: "What does that mean?" "How does it happen?" "My spouse isn't wired that way." "I feel an emotional void, but I don't know where to start."

Trust us, and let's move ahead.

Understanding Each Other

The word and even the concept of intimacy can mean different things to different people. We all have the need, but not everyone knows how to have that need met. Many times women see a need for emotional intimacy, a closeness that is created through sharing feelings. Most women have grown up recognizing and expressing their emotions, though not all.

Unfortunately, men are often brought up being discouraged from showing or feeling emotions, either by direct teaching or through sheer example!

The good news is we can all learn. We can learn to identify our feelings and be able to express and clarify the meaning and understanding behind them. Really knowing what matters to each other and learning how to express our hearts by letting down the walls of fear, insecurity and pain is a process. We have learned many things that have helped this to happen for us personally, but the most crucial is conversation.

Conversation

Conversation, conversation, conversation—with the goal of a complete understanding of each other. With the goal of identifying potential obstacles and seeing the opportunities to find emotional intimacy.

I (Jeff) am not much of a TV person. I prefer listening to my jazz LPs (remember those!) through my vintage audio system, but my wife and ten-year-old daughter love Home and Garden TV! I recently got sucked into watching a show called *Holmes on Homes*. In this show, unsuspecting homeowners have found themselves in homes either partially or fully constructed by less than stellar ethics and even less professional skill. They bring in Mike Holmes who takes a look and then tells them what they need to hear! Getting the house in good shape involves a three-step process of *inspection, demolition* and *renovation*.

What does this have to do with marriage? Your marriage is somewhat of a "construction project." That is, it's something you'll always be working on. To get it in a good place requires the same process.

Inspection

> ...so I went up the valley by night, examining the wall. Finally, I turned back and reentered through the valley gate. (Nehemiah 2:15)

When Nehemiah set out to rebuild the walls of Jerusalem, one of the first things he did was a thorough inspection of the wall. You've got to take stock of where you are! This is all about conversation. This is where the blinders come off and we really see what's there.

A study by American Demographics revealed that working couples spend about thirty-six minutes a day together in cooking, cleaning, shopping, paying bills and demonstrating affection. However, they only spend about twelve minutes a day talking with each other.[1]

From Jeff

Most men are not natural talkers...at least not with our wives! We can talk sports, business or politics with the guys all day long, but when it comes to real heart-to-heart conversation with our wives, we suddenly develop a case of both amnesia and laryngitis. The mind goes blank and the tongue is stilled! I was one of those guys. It wasn't that I was afraid to talk (well, maybe just a little), but it was more that I was clueless.

Then, as we explained earlier, we hit a wall that needed to come down, and we knew it. We were both feeling things that we just were not voicing, and they needed to be said. We needed some serious talk time and I needed to learn how to do it.

From Florence

Conversation can be exhilarating for some and terrifying for others. Being a typical wife, I craved deep conversation. The problem was that I didn't always

---

[1]. American Demographics, reported in *Homemade*, December 1988.

know how to make it happen without it seeming like a police interrogation. I did not want to be a nag or a "dripping faucet," but I needed to talk!

In our house, I'm the one always at the dentist office. Every visit brings a new dilemma! It's not something I look forward to because I know it will mean filling or drilling...and maybe even a root canal! In other words, it's painful but necessary. That's the way conversation can be.

But whether conversation is easy or difficult, it is a vital place to begin the inspection process. Of course, I'm talking about conversation that goes beyond the everyday details of life, which, of course, only seem to get more numerous as your responsibilities increase. Whether it's having more children or job promotions or family dynamics, the importance of going beyond the "air traffic controller" model is imperative.

What do I mean by this? You know: who's driving Billy to soccer, Suzie to ballet, Joey to basketball and Mary to Girl Scouts? Who has the car, who's getting the groceries, who's picking up Grandma, who will answer the voice messages, and when can we talk about the budget?

Our Effort to Make It Happen

One of the many decisions we made was that we had to value our marriage enough to set aside time to talk whether we felt there was time or not...and whether we wanted to or not. Time wouldn't magically appear; we had to want the change in our intimacy desperately enough to make communication happen. This meant sacrifices on both our parts.

We made a decision to sit every night and just simply be with each other. No other distractions! No children, no folding laundry, no doing the bills, no checking email, no watching TV...nothing! Being with each other means sharing our day, our thoughts, our feelings, whatever is on our minds.

Sometimes we'll take a break from talking and play a board game and sometimes talk while we play. We often listen to music in the background and just enjoy each other's company, which leads to a safe time to bring up issues of the heart.

Sometimes we have specific topics we've already mentioned that need to be brought up in "our time" tonight. There have been times when we've laughed till we cried. Other times we've cried and just prayed. We look forward to this time even if we know it will be difficult.

Here are some of the topics we have brought up to help us get closer:

- What are your dreams?
- What are your goals?
- Why are they important to you?
- How can we have these dreams and goals be mutual?
- What really matters to you spiritually, emotionally, physically, sexually?

- Why does something that matters to me not matter to you?
- Here's how I feel about that.
- Why are you afraid to express your feelings about this to me?
- Here's why I'm afraid to tell you what's on my heart.
- Why does this topic affect you more than me?
- Why does this topic bring up so much anger in you?...in me?
- Why do you pull away when I do this?

One of the conversations that got the ball rolling on all this happened one night while sitting on our front porch. We started to talk about future dreams and plans, and here's what happened. Maybe you can relate.

From Florence

My mom came to America from Scotland in 1957. She left behind all of her family and came to the U.S. knowing no one! She eventually met my dad, and they were married. Being a first generation Scot has always been a special part of me. When my mom died suddenly at age sixty-one, I held on even more firmly to her heritage. It was a way of not forgetting her and keeping her alive for my family.

In a conversation with Jeff I mentioned how much I would like to take our whole family to Scotland so that our children can know and feel their heritage and appreciate my mom's roots. Jeff's response was, "We could never afford to do that." All I could hear from Mr. Responsible, Mr. Practical was NEVER!

The tears started to flow, and then the floodgates opened completely! Jeff stared in total confusion, trying to figure out what was happening. What had he said that was wrong? You see, in his experience growing up, having this kind of connection with his family and their culture just didn't exist (for many reasons he will explain). But for me, this was a big deal.

From Jeff

I do remember the conversation and my reaction to it. Florence has much more of a connection to her family heritage than I do. I have no uncles, aunts, cousins, grandparents and besides a brother, a sister and a mom, no blood relatives. Unlike Florence, I know very little about my ancestors and quite frankly, it never meant that much to me! Her desire to go to Scotland and connect her family to ours was to me on the same level as "let's take the family to the French Riviera for a vacation." And of course, in my mind, "We will never afford to do that!"

I totally failed to see the importance such a connection was to her. I didn't grow up with family trips unless the whole family was moving, which we did quite often. (Between the ages of one and seventeen we moved seven times. I attended two different middle schools and two different high schools.) I can remember only one family vacation and that, only a faint memory!

Through this conversation we learned a valuable lesson. We needed to learn *why* things mattered or didn't matter to each other. Why certain subjects were deeply important and others were not. Our talk times allowed us to explore and understand each other's heart! We will get to Scotland as a family one day. It's now a mutual desire that we'll accomplish together.

❊

We can't stress enough the importance of getting this conversation going. We have worked on this goal with many couples over the years. For some it's a slow start. We've had couples report that they sat in silence. Some argued, and some had conversation with themselves, but it's a start! Stay with it. At least you're trying. Like a fine wine, it does get better with time.

Demolition

After Mike Holmes walks through inspecting the house, the real work begins. Demolition! With the ferocity of a hungry bear he starts tearing that house apart. Nothing is spared. Floors come up, walls come down, wiring is ripped out and plumbing gets tossed. All that's bad has to go. An important part of renovating a house is knocking down what's getting in the way of your vision of what the house could be.

Demolition is the fun part. You get to take out all of your inner frustrations with a sledgehammer! Maybe it's a wall that disrupts the flow of the home or dated kitchen cabinets that have to go. When we moved into our home, the first thing we did was have two walls removed. What a difference that made. We still have more to do but it's a process!

We can have so many barriers in our marriage and yet be unaware that they exist. We get used to the flow not being there, but we say, "It's good enough." Knocking down our walls can be what we fear the most, procrastinating year after year. These are not walls of plaster and sheetrock, but walls of sin, dishonesty and fear of rejection and exposure.

We can emotionally shut down and fight to avoid the pain of letting these walls come down and letting our spouse in. We can have wounds that we thought were cleaned and healed only to find there was a little residue left, an infection had set in; the wound was still unhealed.

One of the intimidating walls we had was "past hurts." This was brought out and identified through the inspection, during a talk time. We were involved in a marriage class, and a very simple question in an exercise came up: "Write down one good memory and one bad memory for each decade in your life." Simple enough, after all we've been together so long, we know everything about each other. However, God had a plan to take us to another level of intimacy by demolishing this stronghold of past hurts.

To our complete surprise, a difficult memory from a situation that happened twenty-five years ago came up—a situation we thought was long resolved. A simple exercise brought about the exposure of this infected wound that needed attention. We had to deal with the pain of deceit, immorality and unforgiveness in an area of sin that had been in our lives before we became Christians and before we were married. Even though this was long ago, God knew we needed to flush this situation out so we could build a deeper emotional connection.

Renovation

When Mike is finally finished with all the demolition, the house is barely recognizable! It's a shell of what it used to be, but the owners are happy. Not because of how it looks now, but rather how it will look soon. They know the best is yet to come.

Going through the inspection and demolition in our marriage was a great experience of getting to know each other on a much deeper level. It's not like we hadn't ever talked deeply; we had already experienced some serious life issues together. Both of us had parents who died young and suddenly. Both of us felt the horrible impact drugs and alcohol can have on a family. We had gone deep, but we were able to go even deeper now because we had more knowledge of each other's heart. What an opportunity for intimacy!

Trust God Even When It Hurts

During the hurt, it was difficult to see how God was working. Many times we can't see what God is doing in the moment, but the masterpiece he is creating is revealed later on. We found this to be true.

What comes to mind is the story of Joseph. God had an amazing master plan, but it was revealed a piece at a time. The dream of his family bowing down to him was there in the beginning, but it wasn't completely understood by anyone, not even Joseph. As it unfurled, God was completely glorified!

That's how we feel about our marriage. The vision was there at first, but the pieces have been coming together and revealing the work of art God had envisioned. What he needed from us was what he expected from Joseph: faith, trust and obedience to his word.

Our marriage renovation also reminds us of Joseph's coat of many colors: many pieces coming together to form one in this journey of intimacy. The journey hasn't been predictable or pain free, but the end result *is* a beautiful masterpiece designed by God.

We're sure there are more experiences to be had, more pain, more discoveries and more intimacy. We'll embrace it all! Our marriage is worth it...and so is yours.

Blueprints for Intimacy

Study:
Read these scriptures about intimacy with God, and apply them to intimacy in your marriage: Psalm 145:18 and Psalm 28:7.

Share:
Share with your spouse what you think could be a wall or barrier to your emotional intimacy and what you personally want to do to take that wall down.

Practice:
Begin to make time every day to have quality time to talk. Start with twenty minutes and build from there. Use some of the questions shared in this chapter as conversation starters.

2

The Need for Acceptance

unconditional love brings safety

The need for acceptance is a universal one. We all desire that feeling of someone putting their arms around us and just loving us for who we are, problems and all, failures and all, or as we often hear, "warts and all." As important as this is in friendship relationships, it's absolutely crucial in a marriage. One of the biggest barriers to emotional intimacy is the failure to fully accept the one you're married to. That's not to say we should accept unrepentant sin (in thought or deed), but we must get to a place where we accept each other for who we are, for the person whom God has made.

The reason we don't get to this level of acceptance may be a failure to really know the person we're married to. The end result of this failure is often a conditional love: "I will love you when you change this or that, or whatever...for me." We may not actually say it, but we're thinking it, and more than likely showing it.

Look at the love God has for us. David says, "How priceless is your unfailing love" (Psalm 36:7). David felt confident of that love because he understood that God knew him...really knew him. He was also able to say,

> O LORD, you have searched me
>   and you know me.
> You know when I sit and when I rise;
>   you perceive me from afar.
> You discern my going out and my lying down;
>   you are familiar with all my ways. (Psalm 139:1–3)

An unfailing love is an unconditional love. God can love us unconditionally because he knows us perfectly. The more you know about something, the more you appreciate and value it.

I (Jeff) have a passion for vintage audio gear. Several years ago I picked up a mid-1970s stereo receiver at a thrift store, a Gladding Mark 200A. I'd never seen one before so it caught my eye. (Confession here, my wife and I are thrift store/tag sale addicts!) A quick Internet searched turned up nothing! I thought you could find anything on the Internet. I was now both intrigued and mystified. Somebody out there must know something about this thing.

Finally after repeated searches, I found someone with an original owner's manual. He no longer had the receiver but sold me the manual! I couldn't wait to get my hands on it. Just reading some of the facts and history opened up a whole new world of appreciation for this gem.

The deeper I get to know Florence, the more I appreciate her. There were many years I wished I'd had a "Florence manual," but I'm glad God has now opened up a level of communication between us that gives me all I need to know!

Let Your Walls Speak

There's another HGTV series Florence and our daughter enjoy; it is called *If Walls Could Talk*. In this series the host explores vintage homes with a colorful past. These may be homes once owned by famous (or infamous!) characters or may be the site of a significant historical event. You'll see things like an abandoned home with hidden treasure amongst the trash or money hidden in an attic. Maybe a note hidden in a mirror or a surprise mural behind a layer of wallpaper—history the new owners were not aware of when they bought the house.

In a marriage your past, your history can sometimes be an obstacle or hindrance to intimacy. We can ignore or downplay our past (or our spouse's past) and miss out on a great opportunity to grow closer. To deeply know someone helps to build intimacy. Efforts we make to know each other build a solid acceptance, which in turn builds a "safe place" in our marriage. We begin to feel more of the kind of safety that we experience with God because he knows us completely.

There are few situations worse than feeling unsafe in your own home, so these walls must speak! Your life, your experiences, the highs and the lows, things you've felt and thought. The tears that have been shed and the chains that needed to be broken. The deep secrets of your heart must be revealed.

So again the question: How well do you know the person you're married to? Have you let yourself be known to them?

The more we reveal about ourselves, the more intimate we become. We all have a past, and that past has considerable bearing on our present. There are certain experiences and life events that for better or worse have helped shape our character and personality. Maybe you feel like there's more "worse" than "better" for you. (Praise God for the power of a new life in Christ!) But whatever the case, your intimacy will increase if you can talk about it, and not just talk but learn to accept who you are and who your spouse is...warts and all.

From Florence

What would my walls say? There are so many memories I have. Some great, some not so great. My parents were very loving and nurturing, and they worked hard to provide for the needs of our family. I knew we didn't have a lot, but it was always enough.

Growing up with three brothers, I remember my life being filled with screaming, laughter, pranks and many shouts of "Mom, the boys are teasing me again!!" The fact that I was the oldest didn't seem to make much of a difference either!

I had many dreams of what I wanted to be when I grew up. Dreams of changing the world by becoming a nun or living a life of excitement by being in the circus. Maybe I would be like Florence Nightingale and heal the sick and hurting, or the one I finally landed on after watching many Fred Astaire movies with my dad: the world of musical theater and Broadway!

I was very excited about this dream, and both of my parents reinforced the belief that I could do anything I put my mind to. I was definitely drawn to theater. I loved to sing and dance, and as I look back, it probably became a way for me to escape the painful situations that started happening in my home. It's amazing how clouded that time can be for me with certain scenarios sticking out like flags.

My brother, only a year younger than I, was getting into a lot of trouble in school through drug and alcohol use. There was complete chaos at home. So much arguing and pain between him and my parents. Police at the door, yelling, tears…humiliation, sadness and confusion. I believe the way I dealt with all these very painful experiences was to escape into cheerleading, dance, pursuing my dreams and making sure everybody liked me so I could feel good about something!

I didn't want my parents or my house to be rocked by any more drama. I was frustrated watching my mom trying to lead a dysfunctional family (a role she was not designed for) and failing to see her own co-dependency while my dad held back, not knowing how to lead his family. Both of them were quite naïve about the depth of my brother's drug use and dealing, as well as how it was affecting all of us. My role became the peacemaker where no peace could be found.

As the situation escalated and I watched it deeply affect my parents' lives, I knew I needed even more escape. I decided to move to NYC right after high school to pursue my dream of Broadway and to get away from all this. Little did I know that God would be working in a twist of fate (only to be understood years later) by sending Jeff into my life. I was about to move in a new direction.

We met in a local hangout where I never intended to meet the one I would marry! We began a relationship built on the standards of the world, but we both knew we had something special. Our first date was dinner at an Italian restaurant where we talked about many things, with even a little religion thrown in the mix!

We developed a wonderful friendship, but of course, it could only go so far without a solid foundation, one bigger than us because as we would learn, we could not build it on ourselves. We realized that we had the ability to disappoint each other, with the possibility of hurting each other beyond repair.

As time passed, the differences between us became magnified. Due to my traveling with different shows, we were separated a lot. When you can only connect by phone and that sporadically, and when you only know how to go so deep, the relationship will eventually weaken.

I was with people whom I related to because we enjoyed what we were doing and had similar personalities and basically became a family on the road. When you're in theater, it's like living in fantasyland. The real world is "back home." This can make things more complicated and potentially very destructive if you have a relationship "back home," especially when the boundaries become vague. Being that I didn't have a godly standard at that time, more sin entered the picture.

In hindsight I can see how the differences in our experiences, how we were raised and what we felt we needed as individuals were heightened at this point. We had never really thoroughly discussed the effect our families had on us. We knew what had happened to a degree, some facts, but not at all how it felt or how it had impacted our behavior.

Right about this time I had started to read an old Gideon Bible my dad had given me. I was facing defeats with my career and was becoming someone I didn't want to be inside and out. I started to pray more and found passages in the Bible to comfort me.

Of course as God would have it, he placed disciples in my life at just the right time to guide me and patiently lead me to the truth about God and about myself—also to the truth about the kind of relationship I had with Jeff and what God expected in that.

We had been dating for six years at that point, and the idea of marriage had been swirling around us for a while. Fear had kept me from committing my heart completely to Jeff. As I studied the Scriptures with my friend Leigh, I learned true commitment and that "perfect love drives out fear." I saw how God was working to help us have a very different type of relationship—one built on commitment to him. Of course, Jeff thought this was a crazy idea at the time but later came to his senses!

What I was learning would mean a lot of repenting, clearing my conscience and dealing with who I was. I had to see how my reaction to my past was destroying the present and could ruin the future.

One of the most difficult areas of my transformation was the need to face the truth, tell the truth and be willing to face the consequences of deceit. I knew I needed to open up with Jeff and let him know who I had become, but the fear of rejection and loss was huge! I wanted to escape as I had done many times before, but now I had a reason to face my life and be completely honest.

What allowed me to do this was God's unconditional love! No matter what I had done or who I had become, I finally realized that he would still love me. That doing right by him was more important than the worst reaction I could imagine from Jeff. Now of course this was an extremely difficult conviction to gain, and it came with many prayers and tears.

From Jeff

I have been married to Florence for twenty-five years, but we have been together for thirty-one. Part of the success we've enjoyed in marriage comes from the ability to accept each other's past. I didn't grow up with a very good image of marriage or relationships. My father was an alcoholic for as long as I can remember. (He died violently in 1991 as a result of his alcoholism.) The memories I have are ones of disappointment and dysfunction.

My middle school and high school years were spent largely in a world of frustration, embarrassment, anger and discouragement. My house was not a place to bring friends home to. Things there were much too unpredictable, much too volatile. The risk was too great, the stakes too high. No, this was a place to avoid with any of my friends.

My parents had times of separation and reconciliation, with me, my younger sister and older brother stuck in the middle. It seemed the older I got, the worse things became. When the arguing would begin, I would leave. We were living in Colorado at one point, and I was into dirt bike motorcycles. I would just get on my bike and take off for the trails, anything to escape from home.

The final blow came in my junior year of high school with the inevitable divorce. It was not a "neat" one, if there even is such a thing; in fact it was quite messy! With few options facing us, my sister, my mom and I packed what few things we could into a car. I had just received my driver's license, and I was the one who drove us back to our home state of New York. We had no plan or direction as to where our lives would go next. The promises of financial support from my dad were never kept, and the rest of our belongings were never sent. We had nothing left, and were now facing the daunting task of starting all over.

All this was happening to me at seventeen when

I was going into my senior year of high school. There was no talk of or plans for college. No dreams, no future. We were simply trying to survive, which thanks to the fighting spirit of my mom (a disciple now, praise God!) we did.

I hated my life. I was embarrassed about where we were living and my life situation. I could not have cared less about my high school graduation, and when my friends went off to college, I stayed home bitter, frustrated and envious of their normal lives.

I met Florence in the fall of 1979. She was eighteen with a head of blond curls everywhere. I was twenty-two and still had hair! I laugh now when I look back at the photos. We had an almost immediate bond with her dreams of being in theater and my dreams of being in the music business. Little did I know after that first date, that this was the woman I would marry.

My dating history up to that point was not very impressive. I'd had a few girlfriends, but because of my family past, I was pretty shut down and guarded emotionally. I was so used to keeping people at a distance that I really didn't know how to have a relationship and felt pretty ill equipped to do so.

In spite of that I knew enough to know this was the girl I wanted to pursue, but I had my fears. Would I be able to love someone? Could I trust her? Will I be hurt? Do I have anything to offer her? Will she accept who I am? Will this work?

We began to date and spend a lot of time to-

The Need for Acceptance

gether—more than I'd spent with anyone else, ever! We were having fun being young and in love, and I was optimistic about this relationship as we didn't seem to have any conflict. (How's that for being young and immature!) We spoke about our careers and our future, but as I now look back at it thirty years later, I realize it was a very thin relationship built on a weak, worldly foundation.

That foundation would soon be tested by long periods of separation. Florence's pursuit of a career in musical theater would have her gone for months at a time doing shows around the country.

I was now living in Long Island and going to music school. Mind you this was long before the days of email, cell phones and cheap long distance rates! We would write letters and make a few calls now and then. There was a definite drop in emotional connection, and when we did see each other again, we would simply try to pick up where we left off without dealing with what was really going on in between the times.

We did this for six years and were never really honest about where our lives were. I think we were both wondering where this relationship was going and what our future would be. God would soon change all that!

Florence first met disciples from the then Central Park Church of Christ (now New York City Church of Christ) in November 1984 and began to study the Bible. She got me involved in the spring of 1985 after giving her much grief about it for months. (I was put off by the obvious changes we had to make to deal with the sin in our relationship.)

She was baptized April 7, 1985, and me, May 19. We were engaged to be married and set a date for later that year, but it wouldn't happen before we had some serious face-to-face, heart-to-heart conversation. We had to reveal things to each other concerning our past that directly related to our relationship.

This wasn't easy, in fact it was quite painful, but it had to be done. We realized that the key for us would be the willingness and ability to accept who we were without Christ and how our past history had shaped our thinking. We had to be okay with the person we were moving forward with, knowing that many things had changed, some things were still to change, and there might be things that would never change! Considering all that, is this the person I want to spend the rest of my life with? Can I accept who they were in the past and who they are now?

As we mentioned in chapter one, past events came up in conversation between us many years later, and I realized that I was not fully resolved! This had happened over twenty-five years earlier! We had to talk, pray...talk and pray some more, and it took me reading a journal she kept during her Bible studies to get me in the right place. Let me tell you, things will resurface if you fail to deal with them fully at first.

We said yes to all the questions we had raised about committing to each other, and on a Saturday afternoon in August 1985 we were married.

This practice of acceptance and unconditional love is an ongoing process for us. We are continually learning and relearning how to build a life together. How to take these two different lives with two very different histories and live as one flesh. The older we get the more we understand the Apostle Paul's observation of a "profound mystery"!

Here are some points to consider in building acceptance in your marriage.

Don't Be Judgmental!

Jesus gives us a pretty direct and powerful teaching on this, and it's one that especially needs to be followed in marriage:

> "Do not judge, or you too will be judged, for in the same way you judge others, you will be judged, and with the measure you use, it will be measured to you.
>
> "Why do you look at the speck of sawdust in your brother's eye and pay no attention to the plank in your own eye? How can you say to your brother, 'Let me take the speck out of your eye,' when all the time there is a plank in your own eye? You hypocrite, first take the plank out of your own eye, and then you will see clearly to remove the speck from your brother's eye." (Matthew 7:1–5)

There's a lot in those five verses! We make judgments every day: "That's a great song." "That's not a good policy." "This pizza is the best." "This ice cream is the worst."

We also make judgments about people: "He's the best actor ever." "She's the worst actress ever." "She's a great senator." "He's an awful governor."

We don't feel bad about judging others; we might even say, "It's just my opinion." But for better or worse, our judgments do shape our view of people.

Have we ever wondered what people might think of us? "You do *what* for a living?" "You live *where*?" "What a loser." We might be offended by these thoughts, even though these are only their opinion. Judgment can go two ways. With the measure you use, it will be measured to you.

Now this might not be too terribly important to you, unless you happened to be married to one of these people who are judging you. However, you are married to your spouse, and what he or she thinks and feels is very important. A big part of building acceptance is learning to be non-judgmental in your marriage! It's seeing the plank before you see the speck. There may very well be things you don't get about your spouse, maybe things you don't necessarily like, but before you snap to judgment and become negative, ask yourself a few questions:

- Have I taken the time to understand why he or she thinks or does these things?
- Have I asked the right questions with the right spirit, with all sincerity and with a genuine heart?
- Have I clearly and lovingly expressed how this behavior makes me feel?

- Have I looked at myself honestly to see what I might be doing to bring this behavior on?

Try these and see if your attitude improves!

Don't Try to Fix Each Other

Your spouse will never be perfect and guess what? Neither will you! That's not to say there aren't things that need to change, but in marriage there's a healthy and an unhealthy way to bring about change.

As an evangelist and church leader, I (Jeff) often find myself in situations where I have to confront a brother on something that needs to change in his life. Maybe it's something I see that's destructive to his character, his family or the church. I can't pull any punches, side-step the issue, or sugar coat it. I need to be direct and lay it out; I need to try and fix this. I might even raise my voice a bit, sit on the edge of my seat and look into his eyes with the hope of bringing the fear of the Lord to him. I can do this because at the end of the day, I'm not going home to sleep with him! Don't try this at home!

I think one of the reasons we've been happily married for twenty-five years is that I don't see my role as the one sent by God to fix my wife or her to fix me. We're not in this to fix each other; we're here to love each other. That's not to say we don't address issues or call sin, sin. Quite the opposite. It's just the approach we take that's different.

I prefer to think of it more as "spurring one another on" to change rather than trying to do the repairs ourselves. I'll fix my bike and I might even attempt to fix my Jeep, but I won't try to fix my wife! I love and accept her the way she is, and I trust that God will take care of whatever needs fixing, and use me in whatever way is best.

Build Safety

For me (Florence), a huge part of marriage is building a "safe place," a refuge, a shelter. A place where I can be me and know I've been accepted. Some of the components of building safety that I've experienced are *humility, unconditional love* and a spirit of *perseverance*.

Humility

> Humble yourselves, therefore, under God's mighty hand, that he may lift you up in due time. Cast all your anxiety on him because he cares for you.
> (1 Peter 5:6–7)

Having an atmosphere of humility in your marriage says that you trust God will take control of the situation in due time! He asks us to let him worry about it and reminds us that he cares. When we let pride rule in our marriages, we find ourselves fighting God, and he simply can't work there. He'll oppose us.

Have you ever found yourself hitting a wall? There's pride in there somewhere, and the safety won't be felt. God wants us to know that he cares and he sees what's going on. We need to let God be the one who leads us in conversation. Let God be the one we go to for words to use as we talk to our spouse when things get challenging.

Trust God with the things you see in your spouse that need attention, and ask for his help to accept all of who your spouse is.

Unconditional Love

> A man's wisdom gives him patience;
>   it is to his glory to overlook an offense.
> (Proverbs 19:11)

I love this scripture. It takes so much wisdom to be patient. Safety is built when there is a mindset of "I'm willing to overlook things." When we create an atmosphere of nit picking and negativity, love flies out the window!

I am grateful that God has been patient, loving, kind and tolerant with me, that he has loved me and overlooked so many of my mistakes and sins. This doesn't mean he doesn't deal with me, but he deals with me in love:

> Or do you show contempt for the riches of his kindness, tolerance and patience, not realizing that God's kindness leads you to repentance? (Romans 2:4)

Didn't God's kindness move you to change, especially when you first started to read the Bible and saw who you were and saw much that needed to change? Didn't his patience keep you going as you struggled to clear yourself? Didn't his tolerance fill your heart with determination to do what's right when you tripped over yourself trying to repent of your sin? God's kindness leads you to repentance!

Our patience, kindness and tolerance toward our spouse, our unconditional love, will build safety. We will both live in a place where we feel safe to change.

Perseverance

> Love always perseveres. (1 Corinthians 13:7)

We can tire easily. We can become weary of doing good. Sometimes we think, "I'm too tired to keep fighting for this relationship. I can't keep going; it's too tough" or "Am I the only one trying here?" In order to build safety in your marriage, both need to have the attitude of "I will not give up on this no matter how hard it gets." Remember Jesus who persevered for you and gave you hope and a safe place. Listen to David as he looked to God for refuge and shelter:

> For you have been my refuge,
>   a strong tower against the foe.
> I long to dwell in your tent forever
>   and take refuge in the shelter of your wings.
> (Psalm 61:3)

In our marriages, we need to be this type of refuge and shelter for each other.

Blueprints for Intimacy

Study:

Read Colossians 3:12. What "article of clothing" do you need to see more of in your relationship? Is there a grievance you need to be honest about or something that needs to be forgiven?

Share:

Talk to your spouse about two aspects of your character that you want to change and that you need to be continually aware of. Share with your spouse one or two events that had the greatest impact on your character or emotional makeup before becoming a disciple.

Practice:

Pray together every day to understand each other from the "inside out." Write a card or letter of gratitude for the differences you see, and express how those differences add to the quality of your marriage.

3

I'm Going In

the challenge for men to go deeper

This chapter is from me (Jeff) to the husbands out there. If you are a Christian, odds are at some point you've studied Ephesians 5:22–33. (If your Bible is nearby, take a look at it.) Maybe it was in your pre-marriage counseling. Maybe your post-marriage counseling. Maybe the preacher stood right in front of you at the ceremony and went through this word by word to be sure you got it! I know as a minister, I've done all three.

To me, these are some of the "must know" verses if you're going to have a successful Christian marriage. They speak to the roles and responsibilities of husbands and wives.

One thing that always grabbed my attention about these admonitions is the number of words! I find it interesting that the husband gets exactly twice as much direction as the wife. Go ahead and count. She has fifty-one words of direction and he, 102…to the word—at least in the NIV.

Why is it that the husband has double the words of instruction? Although both husband and wife share in the responsibility for a great marriage (Ephesians 5:21), it's the husband who leads the marriage. That's not my idea; it's God's! The wife is given a charge to submit to her husband.

Making Submission More Appealing

For many women being submissive is tantamount to a fifteen-hour labor with no medication! Submission has a bad rap these days, and I can understand why. A quick spin through the TV dial says it all. Look at the way husbands are portrayed: bumbling fools, insensitive clods, workaholics, spineless, inept men who act more like giant-sized boys than the leader of the family.

Unfortunately, *Married with Children* is too often reality TV, not sitcom! What wife in her right mind would want to submit to that?

Men, I think our wives would have less hesitancy in submitting to and respecting our leadership if we led the marriage the way Jesus leads the church. Ask yourself: "Am I doing all I can do to make her radiant? Glowing?" "Do I put her needs above my own?" "Am I devoted to helping her feel secure and well taken care of?"

These areas are my responsibility—all 102 words' worth. The better job I can do with this, the stronger my marriage will be. In the book of Proverbs, Agur son of Jakeh seems to have a good read on this. Take a look:

> Under three things the earth trembles,
>   under four it cannot bear up:
> a servant who becomes king,

> a fool who is full of food,
> an unloved woman who is married,
>   and a maidservant who displaces her mistress.
> (Proverbs 30:21–23)

This wise man knew what he was talking about when he deplored the situation of a married woman who does not feel loved. What your wife wants most from you...is you! This trumps everything else. You can be struggling financially, the house can be falling apart, and the car can be on its last mile, but if your wife feels and knows that she is truly loved by you, all is well with her soul. Now comes the question. "Just how do I get there? How do I become that husband?"

Making Your Wife Feel Loved

You've got two things to consider: *quality* and *quantity*. Being the husband God calls you to be, the husband your wife needs you to be, requires a deep commitment and serious investment. Not only in the quality of time invested but in the quantity of that time. In both cases, you're going to have to dig deeper.

This is probably not a new revelation to you. Look at the things you love, your passions in life. Maybe it's your career, a hobby, your golf game! Look at the quality and quantity of time invested to be successful. Should your marriage be anything less? No! In fact, the investment should be much greater. You may lose interest in a hobby or change careers, but your wife is for life. Give her the attention she deserves.

Quality Time

Let's begin with the "quality." One of the big challenges for most men is to take it deeper emotionally—to go beyond scratching the surface and get down to where the two become one; that place where the real intimacy is found. It bewilders us, scares us, embarrasses us and intimidates us, and too often the end result is that intimacy eludes us. While our wives are looking to us for that connection, we seem to have a hard time delivering.

Now you can either fold right here and say, "Well, that's just the way I am" or you can say "It's not the way I want to be" and change it. If you're still reading at this point, my guess is you'd like to change it, so let's get to work.

What Needs to Change?

Before you can change anything, you have to be aware of what needs to change. I'm an avid mountain biker. I've even tried my hand at racing. I spend enough time on my bike to know it very well. I know how it handles and how it responds to different terrain. I can always tell when something is wrong... when the "feel" just isn't right. I might not know right away what the problem is, but I know there is one. It may be tire pressure, suspension adjustment, drive train glitch, or maybe a slight bend in the wheel. Whatever it is, I have to find it.

Remember the "inspection" step in chapter one? That exercise led you to look at your marriage; now it's time to look at you. But before we look at you as a husband, let's look at you as a man. This was one of the most important and eye-opening exercises I have ever done.

I didn't do it alone. I had help from some great men in my life as well as a book titled *Wild at Heart* by John Eldredge. Emotional intimacy in your marriage will only happen when you are really able to get in touch with your own emotions, however bewildering, scary or intimidating that might seem to you right now.

Seasons of Life

One of my favorite things about living in the Northeast is the changing of the seasons. Every four months we enjoy a complete change of climate and scenery. Just when you've had enough of the season you're in, it changes!

We all go through seasons of change. We grow up, we mature, we go from one station of life to the next. We learn what we need to learn and we move on.

My older son recently graduated from college with a degree in health promotion. He is now out of school and entering a new season of his life, one of resumes and interviews. How excited he was when he called me to announce he had landed a job in a hospital in Atlanta. He is also now engaged to be married to a wonderful young woman. To me it seems like he just finished playing little league baseball. Oh how the seasons change!

The period of 2005–2006 was a season of change for me. We had just gone through a very turbulent time in our church, and as the evangelist, I was feeling it deeply. It's as though God had hit the pause button and everything was in a state of suspended animation. This time of reflection in the ministry also gave me cause for personal reflection. Not only was I concerned about where the church was, but also where I was.

Around this time several of us in a men's group decided to read *Wild at Heart* together and to discuss what we were learning about ourselves. I had already read the book years earlier, and frankly, it had little impact on me. (I guess that was a different season.) This time around would be different. As the autumn leaves were falling all around me, I realized I was also ready for a new season of change in my life.

The Impact of Your Past

As I shared in chapter two, my formative years were not easy. I know I'm not the only one who would say this, but I wonder how many of us have taken the time to stop and look at the impact of these years on the rest of our life? We tend to want to dismiss or ignore the hurts from the past, but the truth is, how you were raised and the environment you grew up in play a larger role in who you are now as a man than you might think. And, of course, who you are as a man influences who you are as a husband.

One of my biggest personal struggles has always

been emotional intimacy. It has affected every relationship I have ever had. Out of fear of exposing what my family was like, I kept all relationships at a distance. I was well protected! I made sure no one got close enough to enter my world. This included friends, girlfriends, teachers, family...anyone.

I did not have a close relationship with my father. I don't remember him coming to my baseball games or any special events. As I got older, my dad made some attempts to create a bond. He was into antiques and especially antique firearms.

When I was in high school in Colorado, he would take me with him to gun shows for the weekend. I never really had much interest in them, and he seemed pretty focused on what he was doing once we got there (and not very focused on me). We would sleep in the car or sometimes in the venue where his table was set up.

I remember he would always drink a lot at these things. To me, this was not forging much of a bond! We never seemed to be able to get close.

I shared earlier about one memory that is firmly etched in my mind: the day my mom, my sister and I left Colorado after the divorce to move back to New York. I was sixteen and my sister was fourteen. Our dad barely said anything to us. He just let us go as though it didn't bother him.

I remember packing our things, whatever would fit in the car, and driving off. There was such a lack of emotion. I don't remember him trying to explain anything. This was just how it was. Emotionless. The message to me was "I don't really care about you; you're on your own now." I wondered how much I really meant to him.

I remember the drive from Colorado to New York. My mom didn't want to drive, and I had just received my license. I drove the entire way. I had feelings of anxiety and frustration. I felt responsible for my mom and sister, yet totally inadequate and unprepared for the task.

The drive to New York was a real test. "Do I have what it takes?" I think my whole life has been a question of "Do I have what it takes?" I've always had to figure out things for myself: relationships with women, college, finances, career, even something as simple as fixing things. I've always wondered if I "have what it takes."

I carried all this in my heart for many years. I would go from hurt to bitterness to anger to sadness then cycle all through them again. "Why didn't he care more?" "Why didn't he provide for us?"

I forgave him at my baptism in 1985 but did not speak to him until December 1990. We made plans to see each other and for him to see my family in the summer. That would never happen. Tragically, he took his own life in January 1991. The last time I saw him was at the funeral home. There was no memorial, no service...nothing. In a rather strange way, I felt cheated again.

So what does any of this have to do with my marriage, with your marriage? Everything—because it has to do with how we have been shaped as men. I've learned so much about who I am now by taking the time to look back at who I was. I see patterns of behavior that were second nature to me then that can be very destructive in my marriage: independence, insecurity, selfishness, moodiness, aloofness and that nagging question: "Do I have what it takes?"

It has helped me to understand what the apostle Paul said in 2 Corinthians 5:17: "Therefore, if anyone is in Christ, he is a new creation; the old has gone, the new has come." I have the confidence that in Christ, I do have what it takes to be a solid man, to be a great husband.

A Life Plan

The upside of all this navel gazing I've done was a pretty clear picture of who I had become and even more so, who I wanted to become—as a husband, as a father, as a man. To help me out, I set out a few years ago to put together a "life plan" to get me going in the right direction.

In 2 Thessalonians 3:6–15 Paul speaks to not being "idle." The word as used here means "disorderly, disorganized, unfruitful, unproductive or ineffective." I didn't want to have this type of character in any area of my life—and certainly not in my marriage. But I could clearly see areas in which I had some of these negative traits.

I identified four areas to work on: *career*, *family*,

marriage and *personal life*. By design I didn't choose "spiritual life" as one of the categories as I want to make it my goal to be spiritual in all areas. For the purpose of this writing, I'm going to limit my focus to marriage and personal life. These were the questions I asked myself and began to work on:

For My Marriage
- What are our strengths and weaknesses?
- How do we keep growing and staying deeply in love?
- When the kids are out of the house, what would I like our relationship to be like?
- How will we spend our time together?
- What do I really want to do with Florence?
- What are the fun parts of our marriage?
- Where do we really connect?
- How do I keep it fresh and alive?
- What tears us down; what do I need to avoid?
- What can we offer to others?
- What is our anchor?
- What will really make us happy, and what will it take to get there?

For My Personal Life
- Who am I now and who would I like to be? Are they the same? Why or why not?
- What will it take for me to become the man I want to be?
- What changes do I need to make?

- What "course shift" has to be made?
- What are the defining characteristics I want to be known by?
- Which ones do I have now, and which ones still need to be developed?
- What about my relationships? I want strong peer relationships with men who are at my stage of life. Men I can relate to and bond with. Who will be my peer relationships through the second half of my life?
- What do I need and want in a friendship like this?

Four Areas of Focus

Spending quality time with your wife will not come easy. The things we treasure the most usually don't. Here are four things I pray about and work on to help get me there:

Great Faith

I'm reminded of the story in Matthew 17 where the disciples failed when trying to heal the demon-possessed boy. The boy's father complained to Jesus: "I brought him to your disciples, but they could not heal him."

Is that true? Were they really unable to heal this kid? The truth is, they had all the power they needed. In Matthew 10:1 we are told they were given authority to drive out evil spirits and to heal every disease and sickness! Jesus nailed it when he told them they were unable to do this "because you have so little faith."

Faith is always the deciding factor, the defining moment. Faith is where the rubber meets the road! Do you really believe you can be a man confident in who you are, and a husband deeply emotionally connected with his wife? Just like those disciples, you do "have what it takes"; you just need the faith to follow through.

Jesus went on to say to them,

> "I tell you the truth, if you have faith as small as a mustard seed, you can say to this mountain, 'Move from here to there' and it will move. Nothing will be impossible for you." (Matthew 17:20)

What is your mountain? What is stopping you? Remember that in Christ you are a new creation, with all the power of the Holy Spirit working for you! Whatever it is—fear, intimidation, memories, insecurity, pride, embarrassment—have the faith that God will move these mountains aside and you will be the emotionally mature and connected man you want to be!

Personal Discipline

How good are you with the details? Most of the things we fail at are not due to a lack of talent, or skill, or even hard work. We often fail because we fail with the details!

Jesus asked the disciples to prepare the room for the last supper. Imagine if they had dropped the ball and forgot the bread! Our communion services might be totally different today.

Details are important. I love the story of the Good Samaritan in Luke 10. It's a case study in detail! He stopped, bandaged the wounds, secured the injured man on the donkey, brought him to the inn, paid the guy at the front desk, promised to check in on him on his return trip and to pay more if needed. Love is in the details!

Your being this man and husband you want to be is dependent on the details. Organize your time well; let your wife see you are on top of things, especially when pertaining to your marriage. Be the one who initiates prayer and talk time. Be the one ready to set up and carry through with a special time together. Let her see that in your personal life, you are making progress because you're a disciplined man.

A Fully Engaged Heart

The key here is passion! What are you passionate about? Truth be told, those are the things you'll excel in. Read through Song of Songs. Solomon had it going on when it comes to passion! His heart was fully engaged when it came to his marriage!

An emotionally connected husband knows his wife, inside and out. He knows how she feels by simply a look. What she's thinking without saying a word. There is an unspoken language you both know. If you don't know that language, learn it! Let her know that next to God, she is the most important person in your life.

Peer and Mentoring Relationships

The Bible is full of passages about "one another" relationships for a reason. We need each other. Men, you need other men in your life to help you as a man and as a husband. We all have blind spots—weaknesses we can't or won't see. If left unattended, these weaknesses can ruin your marriage and take you out! That's why we all need another set of eyes and ears to help us with what we're missing. (And let's be honest; we can miss a lot!)

As Solomon says, "Pity the man who falls and has no one to help him up" (Ecclesiastes 4:10). Reach out for a helping hand. Extend a helping hand! Get those men in your life!

In this section I have shared some of the decisions and goals that have helped me grow as a man and as a husband. Going after these has helped me spend quality time with my wife, to be closer and more emotionally intimate with her. Trust me, this was time well spent, and I would urge every man to invest this kind of quality time in yourself and your marriage.

Quantity Time

And then there's the matter of "quantity." How much time do I need to invest to be a great husband? (We men like to quantify everything, don't we?) Let me say that I think quality time is more important than quantity, but you have to invest a certain amount of time to see anything great happen.

Men, you carry a heavy load and your wife knows

it. Work pressure, family pressure, life pressure—they all compete for your attention and your energy. By the end of the day you've been drained by deadlines, bottom lines, traffic, the dog, the kids, and too often you are on empty by the time you sit down with your wife. What can we do about this?

Let me suggest you do a "life inventory." Look at all the things you do with your time: work, hobbies, recreation, clubs, activities, interests, people, whatever and whoever. What's fixed? What's movable? What's got to stay, and what could go?

A TV show called *Hoarders* centers around people who can't seem to throw anything away! They want to keep everything they have ever owned, and this undisciplined life-surplus eventually weighs them down and in various ways destroys them!

Consider this hoarding tendency in the area of commitments and activities. Ask yourself: "Besides my relationship with God, where is most of my focus? My passion? My heart? Is it my wife?" If you really want to know the answer, ask her! You may need to throw a few things away. You see, you may be lacking emotional intimacy simply because you don't make the time. Marriage is a huge investment. Respect this truth and put in the needed time.

Remember Ephesians 5, men. God has given you a charge to lead your wives and lead your marriage. Your wife needs you to be strong, yet sensitive. Confident, yet humble. Focused, yet flexible. She wants to look up to you. She needs to be led by you.

Deal with the intimacy killers in your marriage: impurity, laziness, selfishness and anger. She needs to know that you are determined to build a strong emotional bond with her. Take the lead! Rise to the challenge! Make a decision now: "I'm going in! No matter what I've been through or will go through, my marriage will rise to the top and flourish!"

That's the husband God made you to be.

Blueprints for Intimacy

Study:
Study through the Song of Songs. Look at the depth of emotional intimacy a husband can have with his wife. See yourself getting to that point!

I would also you suggest you read *Wild at Heart* by John Eldredge and begin working on the "field manual." I believe you will find this an invaluable aid in breaking through intimacy barriers in your life.

Share:
Talk with your wife about the things you are learning about yourself. Although some things may be painful, the end result will be worth it.

Men, even though this chapter was addressed to you, it would help both of you to respond to the questions on pages 62 and 63.

Practice:
Make whatever changes you need to in your schedule, daily routine or habits to make your marriage a priority. Let's see that "fully invested heart."

4
Worth More than a Ruby
being a noble wife to your husband

As I (Florence) sit in my hometown library trying to pray, meditate and ponder on what I want to communicate to the women in this chapter, thoughts flood through my mind. I glance to my left and on the shelf is a book: *What Men Want.*

That's it! What does my husband want? What does my husband need? How can I fulfill my role as his wife? These are the questions that nag us as wives. We are chosen by God to be our husband's missing rib to complete God's creation. What an enormous task!

The Scriptures indicate that it's hard to find a woman with noble character:

> A wife of noble character who can find?
>   She is worth far more than rubies.
> Her husband has full confidence in her
>   and lacks nothing of value. (Proverbs 31:10–11)

But when a guy does find one, she is worth more than rubies. Rubies, a precious jewel! That's what I want—to be valuable and precious to God and to my husband. What men want is to have "full confidence" in their wives—confidence that they will seek to live in a way that brings blessing to their marriage. The primary thought I hope to communicate through this chapter is how important it is to continue growing in our character. Constantly aiming for that nobility!

My thoughts now shift (which frequently happens) and I'm thinking about the fact that my firstborn son, Taylor, is newly engaged and about to embark on this amazing journey of marriage. I think about how much more prepared he is than Jeff and I were. Having been a Christian for eight years with many deep relationships and mentors to guide him, he is off to a good start.

Recently, Taylor shared his thoughts and convictions about why he desired his future bride and it has stuck with me. In Genesis, God tells Adam he has made a suitable helper for him so he won't be alone. As John Eldredge in the book *Wild at Heart* put it,

> Eve is given to Adam as his *ezer kenegdo*—or as many translations have it, his "help meet" or "helper." Doesn't sound like much, does it? It makes me think of Hamburger Helper. But Robert Alter says this is "a notoriously difficult word to translate." It means something far more powerful than just "helper"; it means "lifesaver." The phrase is only used elsewhere of God, when you need him to come through for you desperately: "There is no one like God of Jeshurun, who rides on the heavens to help you" (Deuteronomy 33:26). Eve is a lifegiver, she is Adam's ally. It is to both of them that the charter for adventure is given. It will take both of them to sustain life. And they will both need to fight together.[1]

---

1. John Eldredge, *Wild at Heart* (Nashville: Thomas Nelson, 2002), 51.

My son sees it this way: As a man he wants to live on the edge, be "Wild at Heart," and he needs a helper, a life saver. Someone that will be there to support him, to help him be who God wants him to be and perhaps rescue him when he gets out in deep water, just like God has done and will continue to do. So what does that have to do with this chapter?

As wives we need to love our husband so deeply that we figure out what he wants, what he needs and who he is so that we take seriously our God-given role to be his helper, his missing rib, his ally, his life saver, his precious ruby. Only then can we provide support, security, appreciation, acceptance, attention, encouragement, affection, approval, comfort and most importantly respect:

> However, let each man of you [without exception] love his wife as [being in a sense] his very own self; and let the wife see that she respects and reverences her husband [that she notices him, regards him, honors him, prefers him, venerates, and esteems him; and that she defers to him, praises him, and loves and admires him exceedingly]." (Ephesians 5:33, Amplified Bible)

Wow! That's a full plate. Women, this is a noble task given us by God. Let's grab hold of the challenge.

Checking Our Hearts

To help with this challenge of being wives with noble character, let's investigate some areas that have the potential to turn our marriage around. I am sharing from my own experience and not just being theoretical.

To grow in my openness to emotional intimacy in my marriage, I had to ask myself several questions:

- Where do I fall short in meeting my husband's needs?
- How has my past affected my ability to be emotionally intimate with my husband?
- In what ways do I go outside my marriage to get my intimacy needs met?
- What are my priorities as a wife?
- What are the "intimacy killers" in my marriage?
- How can I be open about what I am thinking?
- How can I learn to be submissive in the same way Jesus was?

Where Do I Fall Short?

In Matthew 19:16-22 we see the rich young ruler coming to Jesus, letting him know all the good things he has done, and asking what he lacked. Jesus answered, "If you want to be perfect [complete], go, sell your possessions and give to the poor, and you will have treasure in heaven." Jesus knew where this man's heart needed to be challenged.

Women, where does your heart need to be challenged? In what area are you lacking as a wife? I don't want to just add more to your "be a good wife list," but rather to cause you to search deeper in your heart. Be willing to see where the deep changes need to happen so you can live up to the calling and be a wife of noble character—a wife that that "brings [your husband] good, not harm, all the days of [your] life" (Proverbs 31:12).

The Impact of Your Past on the Present

As both Jeff and I expressed in an earlier chapter, knowing your past and understanding the ability it has to hinder intimacy in the present is paramount! I needed to see that my desire to not "rock the boat" or cause problems originated from things I experienced early in my life. Of course, this stunted the intimacy in my relationship with Jeff.

As the oldest of four, my role was the "peacemaker." I would subconsciously think, "Don't do anything wrong" or "Don't let them know I've done something wrong or that something is really bothering me." Why? Because there was enough drama, pain and struggle going on in our house already. The boat was being rocked constantly, and I didn't want to add more and bring on a tsunami!

In order to keep peace, I either lied or tried to bring joy to our home by being successful. Typically, I would downplay the difficulties in our family to those "outside" because of embarrassment, and I would stuff all I was feeling.

When I started studying the Bible, I began to deal with the impact all this had on me. Ultimately, I would need to have some conversations with my brother James, the one who in my mind had caused all the problems. I asked him to forgive me for hating him, and I let him know that I had forgiven him for very painful things he had said and done. I shared that I wasn't any better than he (though in the past I had thought I was) and that we needed to work on our relationship because it was damaged. I wanted him to know that I loved him, but that I had been hurt and wanted our relationship to be different.

Learning how to reconcile and have true peace in my heart had only come from understanding God's grace for me. Many more years of painful times followed this conversation with James, but the most excruciating was his death from drugs and alcohol at age thirty-six.

Of course, this was extremely difficult; no one can be prepared to see their younger brother shortly after he partied himself to death! When I was let into the emergency room to be with him, I hugged him, yelled at him and cried in deep sorrow for the incredible loss of life.

At his funeral, I was able to share the truth with an overflowing room of friends and family—the truth of the pain and joy we had experienced with James. No more avoiding the pain, no more embarrassment, no more "peacemaker"—let's just face the truth. The boat probably got rocked that day!

So what does this have to do with being a godly wife, a wife of noble character? All of this and more impacted how I would function in my role as a wife. In my marriage I was determined to "keep the peace," which resulted in me avoiding conflict and agreeing that arguments were resolved when in my heart they weren't. Not always wanting to deal with reality, I convinced myself that all is okay, just move on, don't "rock the boat."

It is easier than we think to carry into our marriage the role we played in our family growing up. Who we were, how we fit into our family, what we saw, heard or felt can get dragged in and can have a negative impact on our marriage.

So much of the pain of my earlier years was held captive deep inside, just waiting to be dealt with. Some issues I dealt with when I first became a disciple; other pieces of me became clearer as I have gone through new seasons of life.

I know that there is a lot of secret hurt and pain in many women's lives that hold them back from the intimacy they so desire! It might be sexual, emotional or physical abuse. Or dealing with a parent who was more a child than a parent. Or never feeling like they could be good enough, and therefore, dealing with huge insecurities.

Unless we identify whatever has caused us pain and bring it into the light, it will affect the level of intimacy we have with our husbands. We can gain wisdom by looking back, confronting our pain, and learning where God wants to take us. I wanted my focus to be on my present and future, but looking back has been necessary, and it may be for you too.

Getting Our Emotional Needs Met

Let's talk first about "going around" our husbands to get our emotional needs met. Sometimes developing intimacy on an emotional level can seem so difficult. It can be time consuming and complicated, as if you were tackling a new language, a sport you've never participated in, or cooking for Bobby Flay's throwdown!

Sometimes we can get discouraged because we have tried multiple times to connect with our husbands emotionally. It feels awkward for us and for him; it can seem like it's not worth the work! Without even realizing it, we can get our intimacy needs met by our girlfriends, our children, our pets, and at worst men from work, school or our neighborhood.

We need friendships beyond our husbands for sure, and I'm so thankful for all my girlfriends—especially those "forever friends" that I couldn't live without. But we should not seek emotional intimacy with others at the expense of trying to connect with our husbands. This can happen more easily than we think and with totally pure motives.

I've talked with many women and asked them why they thought we have the tendency to seek intimacy from others more than from our husband. Here is what I heard from a couple of women:

First woman

For me it is easier to connect to other women because I don't live in fear that they will stop loving me or have less esteem for me. For example, I won't tell my husband my exact weight or that my weight sometimes makes me sad and embarrasses me. That's something other women can sympathize with, but I am concerned that telling my husband will only make him think less of me and more of other women. I share with him that my weight concerns me, that I want to eat better, exercise, etc...but not the depths of where it takes me sometimes.

In many areas it's as if I want to maintain a certain image with my husband that I don't need with my friends, yet I know that true intimacy asks that I take off the veil and let my real self in all its vulnerability show through. When that happens with my husband, it's always a victory.

Second woman

My children can easily become my focus and priority. I can quickly fix a fall, settle a disagreement or cheer up a sad child with a hug, smile, tickle or even a quick joke. My emotional connection is not very deep, and I also get the reward of I "fixed" it.

With my husband it takes much more patience, time, energy and focus for me to get deep with not only how my husband feels but even more so, how I feel. It is so easy to just go, go, go with the tasks of the day...kids to school, housework, errands, meals, play dates, etc...that I need to stop and be still so I can figure out how I am doing myself to be able to share that with my husband. It can't be mindless and habitual like brushing my teeth. It takes effort and thought, humility and selflessness.

When I don't feel emotionally connected, I physically pull away and then the cycle continues. What has been helping me is making sure I spend alone time every day with God—prayer walks, sometimes a longer shower, or even arriving at an appointment early so I'm not interrupted by the kids. It really helps me let go of any stresses so that I do not take them out on my husband, which enables me to be available for him emotionally.

Do you hear yourself in anything these women shared? In my marriage it happened gradually. It wasn't a complete 180-degree scenario. As I would try to connect emotionally with my husband and not get back what I desired or thought I needed, I ended up relying on close relationships with women. I would tell them all my deepest thoughts and feelings, or I would tell God. That is not wrong within itself, but my role as a wife is to try to connect on an emotional level first with the one I was given by God—my husband.

I went around my husband because of my false perception of his inadequacy to connect, instead of opening up my heart more to him and fighting for what we both needed.

Getting started isn't always easy! We gave one couple the advice to turn off the TV completely and to put the chores aside for a time to connect emotionally (to communicate). Their response was, "What will we talk about?" And they were dead serious.

It can be scary, but wives, we must fight to build intimacy. We need unrushed, focused time together to talk so we can defeat Satan's plan to have us give up and go elsewhere. We must decide as wives to not go around our husbands and take the easier route, but instead, to be patient and persevere in connecting emotionally with our husbands—indeed taking the road less traveled...and as Robert Frost says: it will make "all the difference."

What Are My Priorities?

On another note, it's crucial that we evaluate our priorities to see how they are impacting our marriage. When Jesus challenged the rich young ruler, he called him to evaluate his priorities. Was it going to be his possessions and wealth or Jesus? What is your priority? What can tend to steal or demand your time, energy, attention, and even your heart away from your husband? What do you place the most importance on?

You can figure out the answer to this question by the sheer amount of time and energy you put into it. What is trumping your marriage? What have you allowed to take over in your heart? It can be so subtle; it can start off so innocently, and then you turn around one day and see how far off the road you've gone.

I know this first hand because this is how it happened with me. My marriage stopped being the priority, and everyone else's needs became more important. Whether it was my children or the women I was serving in the ministry, their cries became louder than the voice of my husband. They were louder than the voice of God saying, "Florence, there is one thing you lack."

We can get so off track and so entangled in what we think is more important. What does God say about this situation? "Let us throw off everything that hinders and the sin that so easily entangles" (Hebrews 12:1).

What is hindering you as a wife? What sin is entangling you, causing you to feel hopeless, faithless and maybe even angry about the role God has given you? Maybe you're at the point of giving up on your marriage: "I guess this is how it will always be," your heart cries out!

Sin destroys intimacy, period!

Sin destroys intimacy in our relationship with God, so that the bond is weakened and distance is created. The same thing happens in any human relationship where we allow sin to enter.

The importance of identifying the sin, confessing and getting the help we need to overcome is crucial. I know it was imperative for me to identify the real issue. What sin had I allowed to creep into our marriage?

Intimacy Killers

Here is what I found were the "intimacy killers" for me. I'm hoping you will be able to see yourself and be able to identify your own. Be careful not to flatter yourself so that you can't see your sin because as you know, it is always easier to see your spouse's shortcomings than your own. Let the psalmist David, a man after God's own heart, keep you honest as you search your heart:

> An oracle is within my heart
>   concerning the sinfulness of the wicked.
> There is no fear of God
>   before his eyes.
> For in his own eyes, he flatters himself
>   too much to detect or hate his sin. (Psalm 36:1–2)

For me it was necessary to examine my own heart and get honest with myself first, then get honest with Jeff. He needed to know what I had become convicted of, what sins had I allowed to creep in and set up shop! Below I will share about two that I identified: being deceitful and being unsubmissive.

Being Deceitful

The first one I needed to deal with was deceitfulness. I had not been totally truthful about many thoughts and feelings that I had kept locked up inside. I had been so entangled by fear. I was afraid to reveal my ugly thoughts, my hurts and pains, my concerns, and my deepest emotions. I was very fearful that I would hurt him with all that was stored in my heart.

How backwards I had gotten in my thinking when I knew full well that "the truth sets you free." Fear can be so crippling. I had to see the lies I was believing so that I would stop justifying myself by saying, "It's not that big a deal" or "It's really not that important that I express this to him."

Once I identified what was happening and was open about those hidden thoughts and feelings, I experienced true freedom. It was an amazing and refreshing feeling. I decided that this intimacy killer could no longer exist in my marriage, and I allowed the truth to set me free.

Now a word of caution here! Honesty for the sake of honesty is not always best. You don't need to share every hurtful thought you have about your spouse. For example: not sharing with him if you have been tempted to compare him in some way with other men. Or sometimes finding yourself wishing he was different in some area that is not changeable.

Please get advice from those you are close to and use wisdom. Ask yourself, is this necessary to share; am I building up or tearing down?

Pray! Pray that God will reveal to you your motive for sharing these feelings or thoughts you have not been open about. At the same time don't allow this to give you a way out of really dealing with the deceit.

Being Unsubmissive

The other area I needed to see with more clarity and make decisions about was how unsubmissive my heart could be. Something that helped me tremendously was studying out some key scriptures in 1 Peter. In chapter three, verse one, Peter challenges the women of that day to be submissive to their husbands so even if they were unbelievers, they would be won over by their wife's behavior.

Peter uses this phrase, "in the same way," so I asked myself: "In the same way as whom? Who was Peter referring to?" Peter had just referred to Jesus and his completely submissive response to his father. In 1 Peter 2:21-23, Jesus teaches us what it means to be submissive through his incredible example. There was absolutely no deceit found in his mouth. He didn't retaliate or fight back. He made no threats and issued no ultimatums. Instead he completely trusted God. That is true submission!

This truly challenged my heart, so now I needed to "in the same way" as Jesus, be submissive to my husband. I began to focus on this passage daily, and it helped me to identify the following intimacy killers and to begin changing in these areas.

Being Dishonest—"No deceit was found in his mouth."

I've already shared some about my conviction in this area. This passage just took me deeper in my resolve. I realized that just giving bits and pieces of what was in my heart to my husband or totally shutting down emotionally was not going to be an option!

Submission isn't being silent, eating my words or biting my cheek. It's being completely honest with full respect and love. There could be no manipulation to get my way, or to avoid talking about what was heavy on my heart.

Being Retaliatory—"He did not retaliate."

You have hurt me so I will find a way to hurt you back. Have you ever thought that way? I sure have. I'll withdraw my love, my affection, and in no way can we have sex! I will not open up my heart and get it crushed. I will not take the risk of feeling embarrassed, ashamed or mad at myself for bringing it out. Wishing I hadn't opened up my heart could no longer be my mantra. When we are hurt, our natural tendency is to retaliate and make the score even. Jesus taught us true submission is not about retaliation, but reconciliation.

Making Threats—"When he suffered he made no threats."

Have you ever made threats to your husband? It is so crazy and embarrassing to admit that I have done this. Have you ever said, "I've had enough," "I'm out of here," "I'm leaving" or "I made a mistake in marrying you"? Have you threatened your husband with words because you were suffering? Maybe you felt unloved, uncared for, misunderstood, taken for granted, the list could go on.

I can remember a night I felt frustrated trying to express my emotions, my deepest soul issues, and we kept going around in circles trying to understand each other. Finally my hands flew up, and I said it: "I've had it; I'm out of here! I'm suffering and I need to leave."

But then I thought *where do I go?* I went as far as the porch, feeling like a complete idiot. Knowing inside I was not being like Christ, but being like him seemed insurmountable in the moment. I came to realize that I wasn't being submissive and ultimately was not trusting God, as the scripture says in 1 Peter 2:23: "Instead he entrusted himself to him who judges justly." I needed to trust God and his ways, being patient that God would help me with my weaknesses and trusting that my husband would see his own.

❃

I now have a greater understanding of why the Bible says,

> A wife of noble character who can find?
> She is worth far more than rubies.
> Her husband has full confidence in her
> and lacks nothing of value. (Proverbs 31:10–11)

This is such a worthy task we have as wives, a role designed specifically for you and me by God. This makes me feel very special.

So what do men want? A wife who they can have confidence in, who understands her role. A wife who will be honest with the deepest parts of her soul. A wife who won't retaliate when she is hurt or threaten when she is suffering, but a wife who will put her full trust in God.

Let's fully embrace our role and live up to our "more than a ruby" status that God has graciously called us to.

Blueprints for Intimacy

Study:
Study the verses in 1 Peter that I referred to and come to your own understanding of submission.

Share:
Have an intimacy-building time with your husband, and share with him your "intimacy killers." How you are going to start changing in these areas?

Practice:
Find a very specific way you can make your marriage and your role as a wife more of a priority than it has been. Pray about it daily with your husband.

5
Not Quickly Broken
the importance of spiritual intimacy

I (Jeff) am really not into numbers. Mathematics has always been my weakness. (I'm so thankful for calculators; I never did understand the slide rule.) My youngest child is in the fifth grade now, and to be honest, I dread her homework more than she does.

I watched an episode of *Are You Smarter Than a Fifth Grader?* once. I never watched it again because I had serious doubts! Like I said, numbers are not my thing and maybe that's a good thing. I don't play the numbers or follow numbers.

A Cord of Three Strands

If I was ever tempted to get into numerology, living next to an astrologist in New York City killed that desire. In front of the shop was a sandwich sign that read "Palm Reader" on one side and "Plam Reader" on the other! Maybe they weren't really into numbers either.

There is one number I like. I like the number three. Three is a nice number, a popular number. It breaks a tie. It gets us going—on the count of three let's all shout, "Three cheers for number three!"

The number three also has significant spiritual meaning. We believe in the trinity: Father, Son and

Holy Spirit. Our kids know about the three wise men (or three wise guys as my boys used to call them.) Jonah was in the fish belly for three days. Jesus rose again after three days, and the Apostle Paul tells us that these three remain: faith, hope and love.

One of my favorite scriptures involves the number three:

> Two are better than one,
>   because they have a good return for their work:
> If one falls down,
>   his friend can help him up!
> Also, if two lie down together, they will keep warm.
>   But how can one keep warm alone?
> Though one may be overpowered,
>   two can defend themselves.
> A cord of three strands is not quickly broken.
> (Ecclesiastes 4:9–12)

I've probably read this scripture at weddings as often as 1 Corinthians 13 or Ephesians 5, usually before vows are shared. The scripture makes the point of how much we need God in our marriages.

As do most of you, we have power lines coming to our house from a pole on the street. There are three lines. A strong steel line attached firmly to the pole on one end and to the house on the other. Wrapped around that steel line are two fragile power lines. The steel line bears all the tension. That's where the strength is. The two other lines depend on that steel support line for survival. Without it, they would quickly fall to the ground.

We've had some pretty severe storms here in the Northeast. Even as I sit at my desk typing this, we are recovering from forty-plus inches of snow (including a blizzard) that has fallen in the past month. I've seen trees come down, but those power lines to our house have never budged. A cord of three strands is not quickly broken!

You may very well be better with your spouse than you are alone, but that's nothing compared to where you are when Christ is in the middle. Give it enough time, and you'll have your share of storms. But without that third strand serving as an anchor, you'll eventually fall to the ground too.

Need for Spiritual Intimacy

So how is the spiritual relationship between you and your spouse? Do you recognize the *need* for a spiritual relationship? Many of us became Christians before we were married. Florence and I were married in the fall of 1985, three months after being baptized into Christ. Ours was the first wedding in the recently planted New York City Church of Christ (or Central Park Church of Christ as it was called back then). Although we had many dating relationship issues to work through prior to becoming Christians, we didn't have any marriage issues! However, I know some couples who were married when they became Christians, and it gave them marriage issues to deal with.

Certainly not all these marriages were "bad," but they were at best incomplete. They were more a cord of two strands, not three. There may have been some strength in the relationship, but it was the cord of three strands that made all the difference. I'd like you to hear from a few of them.

John and Cheryl Rountree

We were married twelve years before becoming disciples and have been married as disciples for ten years. Before becoming disciples, we had a good marriage but were struggling with the pressures of unemployment and parenting challenges. The results in our marriage were anger and blame directed towards each other. We argued often and were not unified in our approach to our problems.

After we were baptized, our problems didn't go away, but how we handled them changed. We began to pray daily for our marriage, our children and our worries of life. We sought help and advice from more mature Christians and surrounded ourselves with disciples.

As a couple, unified in Christ, we became stronger and better equipped to face life's challenges. We finally had a firm spiritual foundation for our marriage to grow and mature and to enable us to raise healthy children. There is more love in our home, hope in our thoughts and hearts, and joy in entertaining others.

Bill and Jeanne Patterson

From Bill: Jeanne and I had been married twenty-four years when we became disciples.

Now after over thirty-seven years of marriage, I look back and can see how the depth of my love for Jeanne has changed. It all has to do with learning about and seeing how Jesus loves us and putting that into practice in my relationship with her.

Love is more than just having someone there to be intimate with and providing them with the necessities of life. Some of the ways of real love are doing and saying things that make her feel special and not because you expect anything in return—other than the joy it brings to you when you see how it makes her feel. There is no one I would rather be with than my wife, and I find no greater joy than to be with her, the one I love.

From Jeanne: Before becoming disciples, we had a good, solid marriage based on love and respect, and were entering our "empty nest" phase. We were uncertain as to the challenges that lay ahead, as this was a new phase of our marriage. When we both dedicated our lives to serving Jesus, we became united in a unique way, as we now have a common purpose in fulfilling the Great Commission and helping each other get to heaven.

Feeling the support we give each other now as Christians, and learning about the "real" mission in our lives has been a remarkable source of comfort and security as we grow older. This mutual growth has inspired us to truly look at our lives, make the changes we need to make, and press onward to maturity.

Tony and Judy Paige

Tony speaking for both: When Judy and I married, we had two different denominational priests deliver our vows. Ours lives were of two different worlds, and we didn't know how to bring them together. We didn't understand the importance of unity and denying the selfish desires each of us were so used to gratifying.

At the time Judy was twenty-seven and very much a corporate diva. I was thirty-six and a NYC firefighter/professional model signed with a prominent talent agency. We decided to marry because Judy was pregnant, and it seemed the only sensible thing to do. Getting married did not bring us any closer, which created a great insecurity in my relationship with Judy. After a year of marriage and the birth of our young daughter, I vowed to leave this marriage.

Fortunately, I was met by an unsuspecting brother who invited me to play basketball, his name was Kevin Garrett. After I had played ball with him and the other brothers for a few weeks, he invited me over for dinner so Judy could meet his wife, Echo. They prepared such a delicious spread of food that we were amazed by the whole experience and wanted to know more about them.

After coming to church, we decided to study the Bible, and six months later, I was baptized and then I baptized my wife that same day. Studying the Bible gave us the foundation we needed to fight off the many temptations that were placed in our lives. When we were first met by disciples we had been married only one year. This February we will be celebrating our twenty-second wedding anniversary.

We believe God had a plan for us when he put great men and women in our lives to show us the meaning of Christ's love. By growing through our many struggles we were able to learn how to bring this love into our marriage and teach it to our four children, three of whom are now disciples, and the youngest is studying the Bible.

It is so important to learn the lessons of God for our lives. Although it has not been easy, we have never been happier.

Jim and Nancy Fuda

In 1975, one year out of college, we started our married life together. Now, after thirty-six years, we look back and see how God has protected us and blessed us over these years. The first twenty-two years, as non-disciples, our marriage grew and was bound by the qualities of trust and commitment.

Our lives were intertwined as two cords together raising children, building careers, and investing in our future. Life had its normal moments and challenges, but the strength of the two cords—trust and commitment—pulled us through.

In 1998, our lives were dramatically changed

as we became disciples beginning a true relationship with God and exposing ourselves to his word and teachings. As our spiritual relationship with God grew, so did our emotional closeness to each other. We have experienced a deeper fulfillment and enrichment of our marriage as disciples and have realized God's commitment of Ecclesiastes 4:9–12: a "cord of three strands is not easily broken." To keep the three cords tightly woven, we often read and study 1 Corinthians 13 to ensure the qualities of love remain in our marriage.

Whether you were married as Christians or not, God is poised and ready to work in your lives right now. He longs to be that third strand in your marriage. There are some things you can do, some steps you can take to ensure you are building that spiritual relationship together.

Man to Man

Let me (Jeff) talk to the men for a bit. Guys, take a look at Genesis 2:18: "The Lord God said, it is not good for the man to be alone. I will make a helper suitable for him." What does that tell you? It's not a good idea for you to be alone! Not because you can't cook or clean up after yourself, true as that may be, but there's a different help you need. It's the help to get to heaven. That's why God gave you a suitable helpmate.

Building Spiritual Intimacy

So now the question is "How do we build that spiritual relationship *together?*" Not just "him and God" or "her and God," but "us and God." You need those three strands. Let's not forget that God created marriage to be first a spiritual union: "Therefore, what God has joined together let man not separate" (Mark 10:9). We can procreate without marriage, but it's the spiritual union we have with God that makes what we have with each other so special.

Many couples we have worked with have a good understanding of the importance of a personal relationship with God. The problem is, they keep it too personal. He has his prayer time in the morning before work; she prays at night while he's catching up on things. She studies her Bible in the morning while he's at work, and he studies at his desk before work begins. He's reaching out to a guy at the gym, and she's sharing with a woman at the book club. He gets with the guys from church on Saturday morning, and she meets with the women Sunday after service. I think you get the picture!

While none of these is wrong or bad, they seem to miss the concept of "one flesh." There is little spiritual time together. I fully understand the challenges of a busy schedule. And in many cases, what I've described might seem necessary. Even with the most challenging schedules, there still has to be time made to spiritually connect with each other.

Experience tells me that often the problem doesn't lie with the schedule but rather with the scheduler! If there's a lack of spiritual intimacy in your marriage, it's probably not due to anything external but rather internal. As with most things, it's a matter of the heart. There's a blockage in the artery that needs to be opened up. You need a clear line of spiritual communication, of spiritual intimacy between you and your spouse. Unfortunately it's a line that's missing in many marriages and has a direct impact on your emotional intimacy.

A study by the National Survey of Marital Strengths using the ENRICH Couple Inventory shows the following results:

- 53% of married couples disagree on spiritual beliefs.
- 48% are dissatisfied with how they express their spiritual values and beliefs. 46% say spiritual differences cause serious tension in their relationship.
- 50% say they do not feel closer because of their spiritual beliefs.
- 48% do not rely on their spiritual beliefs during difficult times.

What this tells me is that a significant number of married couples have problems with spiritual intimacy. Maybe they had it once but lost it. Maybe they never had it at all. Whatever the case, it's not there now.

Fear Is a Deterrent

Look at your own marriage. Is it there? Do you have spiritual intimacy with your spouse? If so, great! (Move on to chapter six and you're good to go.) If not, why not? There may be many reasons why, but one of the biggest reasons I've seen for this lack of spiritual intimacy is fear. What are you so afraid of?

For men much of the fear we feel may actually be insecurity. We've read in the Bible that men are given the charge to be the spiritual leaders in the relationship. Ephesians 5 makes that clear, and while many a godly husband may want to wholeheartedly embrace this, many of them fear *being* that spiritual leader. "Will I be good enough? Smart enough? Righteous enough? Deep enough? Will she respect my leadership?"

I believe what she will respect is that you love her enough to want to lead her spiritually and build a spiritual relationship. Don't fear what you think you can't do. Focus on the things you can do. You can pray together daily. Not just before meals but a meaningful time of prayer where you hold hands and share the deepest things on your heart. You can share what you're learning in your Bible study or what you learned from the Sunday message or the midweek class. This is not a "test time," and you won't be graded on how well you can recall all the details, but it is a time to share how God is moving in your life.

This is a time to explore, learn and grow together. Share your spiritual goals. Share your dreams, but most of all, share your heart. Be excited, be encouraged—just don't be afraid! Remember there is no fear in love, but perfect love drives out fear (1 John 4:18). Let God encourage and equip you to build that spiritual intimacy.

Woman to Woman

Most women crave closeness. We love to know the inside scoop, what's really going on up-close and personal. We want to know all the finer nuances. (Maybe we're just nosy.) How many times have you stood in line at the supermarket and found yourself sucked into the *People* magazine while waiting to check out? Or you've gone to the ladies room with a friend just so you could finish hearing the final details of a story.

My boys have experienced this with me many times. When they would come home from an event, whether it was sports, school, church, a date, whatever…they would brace themselves for the interrogation. "How was it? When? Who? What? Where? Give me the details, every little one."

This was torture for them, but it was torture for me to just get, "It was good." They got some great coaching from their dad who taught them to prepare ahead of time and be ready to give a good but brief summary to satisfy me. I want to know the details of their lives. It helps me to feel close to them.

For me, it's the same with God. Being close to God has taken me years of getting to know him. Through going over and over the details expressed in his word,

I'm trying to grasp him with greater depth of understanding. How he might feel in a certain situation. Why he might respond the way he did in another. I need to talk to God through prayer to attain the closeness I so desire.

Applied to Spiritual Intimacy

What does all this have to do with spiritual intimacy in a marriage? When I think about being spiritually intimate with my husband, I know it will take the same effort and desire for closeness that I have with God and my children. This is a very important element in our marriages that we can't afford to neglect.

I want my husband to know my relationship with God and be able to experience it alongside of him. I think we can have a misconception of what it means to have spiritual intimacy. We can think it only means studying the Bible every day together or doing spiritual activities together, or just being together in church. Yes, these are things we can certainly do, but we can still avoid intimacy *while* we're doing them!

Developing this level of intimacy won't happen simply because we have shared beliefs. I need to consistently share with Jeff my friendship with God, my ups and downs with God, my understanding of God.

As Jeff talked about, praying together helps greatly! When we pray, we are open and vulnerable with God, and this gives your spouse another window into your heart, the good and the bad! It's also helpful for me to know what my husband is struggling with and what he's excited about. What's potentially discouraging to him and how I might help with a scripture, or what new and wonderful piece of God's word he's gained new insight into.

We can't read each other's mind, so these are things that need to be expressed. Sometimes we might wish our husband would be more forthright in sharing his spiritual thoughts with us when we just need to be good at sharing ourselves first and opening up that door for him. You might want to suggest choosing some scriptures to memorize together, letting him know this would encourage you.

Now this is where it's important to say that I don't mean that you need to nag him to accomplish this. We know that doesn't work nor is it fitting. Expressing our desire and need to share our spiritual lives with each other can be done without nagging!

Be careful you don't have unrealistic expectations. Your husband may not be in the same place as someone else's husband with this. Don't compare where he is with where someone else is. Be the helpmate God created you to be and encourage him! If your husband is serious about growing in his relationship with God, he knows who he needs to be and he'll get there. As I mentioned before, it's taken us years of poring over God's word and praying to get to a good place with this. Be patient, but most of all faithful!

It's a Journey

Spiritual intimacy with your spouse is a journey. It does not happen overnight. Enjoy the ride! Think of a beautiful drive where you both are taking in all the scenery, fully engaged in what you're seeing, but seeing it from two different angles, sharing the details with each other as you travel along.

Once Jeff and I traveled down the California coast from San Diego to Mexico. It was fantastic, but I'm sure we both have different memories of the trip that combined make up *our* memories.

For me it was the lobster prepared in a way I've never tasted before. For him it might have been being pulled over by the police in Tijuana. Whatever, these are shared memories that bond us together. Spiritual intimacy involves shared memories of how God has been wrapped around both of us, holding us together, weaving the three strands into a braid that will keep us strong till the end.

Blueprints for Intimacy

Study:
Read 1 Corinthians 13:1–8 together. Apply these scriptures to your marriage. What are my strengths and weaknesses? Be totally open and honest with one another.

Share:
Tell your spouse an aspect of his/her relationship with God you would like to see become more a part of your marriage (e.g., prayer, faith).

Practice:
Make a practical "action plan" to build a deeper sense of spiritual intimacy in your marriage.

6

Don't Settle for Less

having vision for your marriage

There's a scene from the 1954 motion picture *On the Waterfront* where one-time prize fighter Terry Malloy (Marlon Brando) is having a talk with his brother Charley about the tragic path Terry's life was on:

> Charley: Look, kid, I...how much you weigh, son? When you weighed 168 pounds you were beautiful. You coulda been another Billy Conn, and that skunk we got you for a manager, he brought you along too fast.

> Terry: It wasn't him, Charley, it was you. Remember that night in the Garden you came down to my dressing room and you said, "Kid, this ain't your night. We're going for the price on Wilson." You remember that? "This ain't your night"! My night! I coulda taken Wilson apart! So what happens? He gets the title shot outdoors on the ballpark and what do I get? A one-way ticket to Palooka-ville! You was my brother, Charley, you shoulda looked out for me a little bit. You shoulda taken care of me just a little bit so I wouldn't have to take them dives for the short-end money.

Charley: Oh I had some bets down for you. You saw some money.

Terry: You don't understand. I coulda had class. I coulda been a contender. I coulda been somebody, instead of a bum, which is what I am, let's face it. It was you, Charley.

Life is full of "coulda, woulda, shoulda." How discouraging it is to talk with people at the retirement age, a time when they should be able to relax and enjoy life, and hear from them little more than bitterness and resentment. We jokingly call them "grumpy old men" or "mean old ladies," but it's no joke and is really quite sad. A life full of coulda, woulda, shoulda. "I shoulda done more with my life. If I knew then what I know now, I woulda done things differently. I coulda been a contender!"

You don't want to say this about your life one day, and you certainly don't want to say it about your marriage. As I've already pointed out, we have an extremely high divorce rate in this country, but to me what's equally alarming is the number of marriages that stay together but one spouse or maybe even both have lost touch with what a real marriage is or could be. They're more like roommates than a married couple. Some have gone to separate beds and in some cases, separate bedrooms.[1]

---

[1]. There may be some situations where a separate bed or even a separate room may be necessary for quality of sleep. This may be due to a medical condition or a physical disability. These couples do not necessarily have an issue with intimacy. This is not what we are talking about here. We are concerned with couples who sleep separately because of lack of intimacy.

Those are marriages that "coulda been contenders." Could have been great. Could have been growing. Could have been happy, but they settled for less, much less. Not all marriages end in divorce or even get to the point of separate bedrooms, but far too many have settled for less. Why? Look at these scriptures:

> Terah took his son Abram, his grandson Lot son of Haran, and his daughter-in-law Sarai, the wife of his son Abram, and together they set out from Ur of the Chaldeans to go to Canaan. But when they came to Haran, they settled there. Terah lived 205 years, and he died in Haran.
>
> The LORD had said to Abram, "Leave your country, your people and your father's household and go to the land I will show you.
>
> "I will make you into a great nation,
>   and I will bless you;
> I will make your name great,
>   and you will be a blessing.
> I will bless those who bless you,
>   and whoever curses you I will curse;
> and all peoples on earth
>   will be blessed through you."
>
> So Abram left, as the Lord had told him, and Lot went with him. Abram was seventy-five years old when he set out from Haran. He took his wife Sarai, his nephew Lot, all the possessions they had accumulated and the people they had acquired in Haran, and they

set out for the land of Canaan, and they arrived there. (Genesis 11:31–12:5)

What did Terah set out to do? He was on his way to Canaan. God had something great planned for him there. But what happened? He settled for Haran! Now was Haran a bad place? Maybe not, but it's not where God intended him to be. God wanted him in Canaan.

God goes on to tell Abram, "Get up and go! Go to that promised land and I'll bless you greatly." At seventy-five he left, and God did indeed bless him. It's never too late for God to bless you. God has a promised land for your marriage. Maybe you've tasted it; maybe not, but there *is* a place God wants you to find, and when you find it, stay there! Don't settle for anything less.

The Sexual Relationship

As you may have noticed by now, we really haven't talked much at all about sex in this book! One might argue, "Isn't that what intimacy is all about?" Well, certainly sexual intimacy is a part of intimacy in marriage, a rather big part, and there are many great resources you can find to work on your sexual relationship. I would highly recommend reading *The Five Senses of Romantic Love* by Sam Laing available from DPI.[2] Sam covers the topic better than anyone I've seen.

I do however want to share with you the impor-

---

2. Sam Laing, *The Five Senses of Romantic Love: God's Plan for Exciting Sexual Intimacy in Marriage* (Spring Hill, TN: DPI, 2008).

tance of the emotional-sexual relationship in marriage. Often when a marriage begins to sour, one of the first things to go is sex (which I guess is why sleeping in separate beds isn't much of an issue).

Consider the following scriptures:

> ...each man should have his own wife, and each woman her own husband. The husband should fulfill his marital duty to his wife, and likewise the wife to her husband. The wife's body does not belong to her alone but also to her husband. In the same way, the husband's body does not belong to him alone but also to his wife. Do not deprive each other except by mutual consent and for a time, so that you may devote yourselves to prayer. Then come together again so that Satan will not tempt you because of your lack of self-control. (1 Corinthians 7:1-5)

We are sexual beings! To my knowledge, humans are one, if not the only, species that has sex not just to procreate, but because it's fun! Ain't nothin' wrong with that! What a great gift God has given us. Your sexual relationship with your spouse is the only thing you share exclusively with your spouse. Are you making the most of it? Can you imagine it any better, or are you settling for less?

It's a fact: the level of your sexual intimacy is directly related to the level of your emotional intimacy. The deeper your emotional intimacy, the better your sex will be. Sex is a good thing, but can be a great thing! The key is, you must be comfortable talking about it. We not only talk about it, but we pray about it as well. No games, no guesswork, no assumptions, no awkwardness, we get right to the point. It makes for great conversation.

Do you know what your spouse really likes and dislikes? What are his or her expectations? How important is it to know the answers to these questions? Very! Without that information, you're flying blind, hoping for the best. You may come in for a landing, you may not. You may hit the center of the target, you may not. There is way too much potential for greatness here, why take that kind of chance?

Florence has this to say...

As wives, when we read or hear something like 1 Corinthians 7:3-5, we can sometimes focus on the sexual relationship as my "duty" as a wife, totally missing the point! Whether it's feeling sexually fulfilled ourselves or meeting our husband's sexual needs, there is a direct connection to his emotional needs.

Our attitude plays a major role here. This is the easiest area to settle for less. A good sex life is not measured by the amount of times you manage to have sex but rather the attitude of the heart behind it. We can be deceived as women and think that it doesn't mean that much and we can easily do without it. We have to remember that this attitude is not part of God's design and is more the influence of the world than anything else.

That brings me back to 1 Corinthians 7. A few years ago I read this scripture and saw it differently than I ever had before. My perspective had changed. I now saw words such as "mutual" and "devote," "pray" and "Satan." This is something to be taken very seriously.

Hearing from Others

It's often said that there is no substitute for experience, and I (Jeff) believe that. Twenty-five years of marriage and ministry have opened my eyes to a lot. I appreciate people with experience. I want to know that my doctor and my mechanic have been around the block at least a few times before getting to me.

We thought at this point it might be encouraging to hear from some very well respected "veterans" of Christian marriage—people who have made the decision not to "settle." We've asked several couples married as disciples twenty-five years and more to share what has helped them to keep it going and keep it strong. Listen to what this "great cloud of witnesses" have to say.

Sam and Geri Laing

We have found that keeping Jesus Lord of our individual lives is the most important thing in keeping us close to each other. In any situation, if we ask ourselves what Jesus would have us as individuals do and be, then we come together in love in an intimate, peaceful manner. When we become self-willed and self-centered, then our marriage suffers. We have also found that the simple act of praying together does much to keep us close. It is as if we are both as children of God asking our Father to come to us and help us be closer as his children—it is hard to be separate from one another when our Father is the glue!

On a practical level, we try to remain in open communication on the fact, opinion and feeling level on a continual basis. We talk openly and freely, sharing our deepest thoughts, feelings, attitudes and needs. We made efforts to spend time alone away from the house even when we were in the midst of raising our kids. It took effort, but it was worth it. We have worked to maintain the fire and passion in our romantic life, and that also has kept our marriage exciting and strong. We are quick to solve problems, quick to apologize when we are wrong, and do our best to come to complete forgiveness when we have hurt each other.

We try to overcome evil with good by complimenting and recognizing the best in each other, and saying it in words and in writing...all this and more. Marriage is a lifetime of growing and learning, and it is worth every minute of time and effort!

❉

Dave and Kathy Eastman

Kathy and I have enjoyed twenty-seven wonderful years together, and we boil our successful marriage down to one basic principle: a commitment to communication. Early in our marriage, we learned that we had to get out at least once per week, away from the house, with no distractions, and talk until we cleared out whatever was in our "communication file."

This was not a date night; we did that as well. It was a time of focused, scheduled communication allowing us to talk about anything that was on our minds: our schedules, our kids, our physical intimacy, our finances, our dreams, our plans, our division of labor, and on and on. We have taught this for years, and those couples who put just that one thing into practice consistently do better in their marriages.

The challenge with this kind of communication is in maintaining a deep and abiding humility. As a husband, I have to be consistently open to my wife's input, and trust her instincts and observations, especially as they pertain to our communication. Most wise men I know have figured out that communication is often a huge strength in women, and an area of needed growth in men. Wives need to be just as humble, and accept their husband's leadership and observations.

Finally, both husband and wife need to be humble in pursuing good spiritual friendships with other couples who can help us to have healthy communication, keep a spiritual focus and resolve conflict quickly.

Jimmy and Anita Allen

I heard a man speak about how all corporations have a board of directors. They do this because they want wise advice from many mature people to keep their business running effectively. He added, however, that virtually no one does that individually with their lives. I have been very fortunate in my marriage to have a spiritual board of directors watching my marriage and family for over twenty-five years. I have really needed the help, encouragement, challenge and consistency in input. Great friends and mentors like Wyndham and Jeanie Shaw, Al and Gloria Baird, Don and Lee Burroughs, all of the Hartford elders and wives, and others have been God's heroes in my family's life.

In addition to the unbelievable, ongoing aid from my "board," Anita and I have had a regular one-on-one marriage time every Monday for more than twenty-five years. We have used the weekly format of sharing (1) some things that we love about each other, (2) one thing the other person can do better, and (3) scheduling, kids, feelings, etc. It is a consistent time we look forward to every week, and nothing bumps it from the schedule. That priority has allowed us a quality time to talk and keep the possible bitterness issues out and put loads of gratitude in.

Jayson and Laura Colby

When I think of intimacy in marriage, I think of communication. The verse that comes to my mind is Ephesians 4:15: "But speaking the truth in love, we are to grow up in all aspects into Him who is the head, even Christ" (NASB).

In the early years of our marriage we loved each other intensely, but the emotions themselves sometimes undermined the opportunities to help each other grow spiritually.

Even though intellectually I knew that my wife loved me, when she offered "constructive criticism," I would be personally hurt. Sometimes I reacted with anger, other times by withdrawing and shutting down.

In either case, I did not benefit from the applied spiritual wisdom of the one who knew me best and loved me most. I think this is Satan's way of short-circuiting the power that God desires us to have in our marriages. He wants this power to transform us so that we can be a light to others as well.

Thankfully over the years, we have learned to let our guards down and listen to one another when we point out sin or areas of weakness that we could grow in.

Jesus himself was incredibly direct in calling others to change, yet always what the Lord said was done in love. This is the way that God has brought amazing blessings to our marriage, and because of the growth that occurred, also allows us to patiently listen and counsel others in their marriages as well.

❄

Larry and Mary Lou Craig

After forty-one years of marriage, we are having more fun than ever! The most obvious reason for our continuing to grow in our marriage is the individual commitments we have made to following Jesus and letting him change and rule our lives. After many years, though, we have learned a valuable perspective which continues to enrich our lives.

We never cease to be amazed by how different we are! If there are two ways of doing something, we each naturally choose a different way. Our differences can definitely be potentially annoying! We've chosen, however, to relish those differences! We've learned to appreciate and even admire each other's different strengths, different points of view, and different approaches to various situations.

So we see ourselves as a team! We smile at our different ways of doing things. We love that together we are stronger, smarter, more complete and more spiritual than either of us is alone! Truly "two are better than one" (Ecclesiastes 4:9).

❄

Barry and Debbie Holt

What has helped us to stay spiritually and emotionally close over the years? God being the center of our relationship and being united in our purpose in serving him. We are very grateful that God has given us great role models who have been involved in our lives and have shown us how to love, how to forgive and how to extend grace and mercy to each other. We have learned the importance of making our marriage a priority by protecting our times together in the midst of life's busy schedule.

We have made special efforts to stay connected and to keep the romance alive in our relationship through date nights and special getaways.

Lastly, we have found that in giving to others by helping them in their walk with God and in their marriages, we are helped to stay grateful, and spiritually and emotionally connected.

❆

Lincoln and Irene Gifford

Irene and I have our own interests: Irene is involved in music, art, photography, and I like fishing, camping, sports. However, there is nothing each of us enjoys more than spending time together. We like being together, more than anything else in the world! Since the early days of our marriage, we have made the effort to get away for a night or two, several times a year. We found a common interest in kayaking, which we do together most weekends (when the weather cooperates). We enjoy going out to dinner, and we talk regularly. We are great friends, and are thankful to God for the companionship we share.

Another key to our unity is the traditions (or good habits) we have developed. We take a family vacation every year. We eat together every evening, spend regular time with our children, and have holiday traditions.

Finally, when we need help with a disagreement we can't resolve ourselves (which happens from time to time), we get help. We believe that every couple needs help occasionally, and it is critical to get that help so that important issues are always resolved.

Wyndham and Jeanie Shaw

From the time we began dating, we incorporated "spiritual disciplines" in our relationship that we continue to this day. These have served us and our children well. Prayer and planning together is key for us. When we began dating in college, we took a couple hours in the afternoon each week to walk and pray together, in addition to our "Saturday night date." We would ask God to help our relationship be what he desired, to help us be pure, and to use us for his glory. During these times we got to know what was in each other's heart as we heard each other communicate with God.

We have continued this "habit" over the past thirty-six years of our marriage. At the beginning of each week we take several hours to plan our week (making sure we are on the same page with each other in terms of our schedule) and to pray. We evaluate what we have coming up in the week to make sure we spend plenty of time with other disciples, allow time to reach out and to be hospitable, and include time with family and friends.

In this planning time we also discover when our plans and expectations don't match up well. We have learned that missed planning and prayer time can often result in unmet expectations from each other that result in bumps that have to be resolved. Often I (Jeanie) don't know what I am feeling until I begin to pray. In our prayer with each other, vulnerability comes out. We have found that it is hard to come to God without owning our personal responsibility for resolving conflict. It helps us both get humble in our personal communication even if we don't start out that way.

We have been well aware through the years that although we carefully plan, God directs our steps sometimes in different directions from our plans. When we look back at the many ways he has done this, we see times that have been filled with fear and courage; heartaches and inexpressible joy; being stuck in a rut and experiencing refreshing times of growth; exhaustion and exhilaration.

In all of these experiences, the time we spend together in prayer daily, as well as the more extended time weekly, has drawn us closer and closer to God and to each other. To us it is more than a good idea, it is a necessity!

❊

Wow! That's quite a cloud. If nothing more, this sharing alone will keep you going strong!

In 1988 we had the opportunity to travel with a group to Sao Paulo, Brazil, for a week to help with a new church. We had a very busy schedule, and I (Florence, of course) was seven months pregnant. As we were nearing the end of our stay, we all went out to a local restaurant for dinner. I ordered filet mignon because I had never had it before, and we were told the beef in Brazil is some of the finest in the world. (I think the steak was $5.00!)

After you've been exposed to that standard of excellence, it's hard to settle for anything less. Your thoughts always come back to that experience of excellence. Make the decision to experience the best, to go after excellence in your marriage. Once you do that and come to know even moderate success, you will never want to go back to the way it was.

Nobody ever said marriage is easy. If that's what the salesman told you, he was lying. Having a great marriage is work, hard work, but a labor of love. Put the time in, put the effort in, and put the heart in. Fight for the bond, fight for unity. Don't be easily discouraged, and stay at it, pushing forward and refusing to settle for anything less than glorious.

We truly believe that if you build the emotional intimacy your marriage craves, you'll end up with more than you can imagine.

Blueprints for Intimacy

Study:
Read 1 Corinthians 7:3–5 together. Ask yourselves: What is our shared conviction about this for our marriage?

Share:
Talk with your spouse about the areas in which you believe you personally have "settled for less." Discuss your strategy for change!

Practice:
Set aside time to write a love letter to your spouse that reflects some of the concepts you have learned by reading this book. Share your letter with each other.

Notes

Notes

Notes

Notes

Also available from www.ipibooks.com

Spiritual Leadership for Women
by Jeanie Shaw
Price: $13.99

www.ipibooks.com

www.ingramcontent.com/pod-product-compliance
Lightning Source LLC
Chambersburg PA
CBHW030155100526
44592CB00009B/286